ABRAHAM

ABRAHAM

Friend Of God

Abraham - Friend of God
First Ambassador Edition 1993

ISBN 0 907927 86 6

AMBASSADOR PRODUCTIONS LTD,
Providence House,
16 Hillview Avenue,
Belfast, BT5 6JR.
U.K.

Contents

Preface

I am very sensible of the inadequacy of my attempt to conceive, or portray, one of the greatest characters of History. And yet there is one thought pervading the entire narrative, which brings it near to the poorest limner of its noble outlines. Abraham was great through his faith. And that faith was at first but a silver thread, a tiny streak, an insignificant sinew—not stronger than that which trembles in the humblest and weakest reader of these lines.

But wherever faith is, it is the link with Omnipotence; the channel for the Divine communications; the wire along which the Fire of Heaven may travel. And as it is used according to the promptings of the Divine Spirit, and in obedience to his commands, it will grow. It grew in Abraham. It will grow in us.

To trace the laws of that growth, and its gradual increase, for the encouragement of those who by faith are the children of Abraham, and who long with intense desire to emulate their great progenitor, until they can remove mountains of difficulty and achieve apparent impossibilities, has been the great principle on which these pages have been prepared.

F. B. MEYER

I

The Hole of the Pit

The God of glory appeared unto our father Abraham, when he was in Mesopotamia, before he dwelt in Charran; and said unto him, Get thee out of thy country, and from thy kindred, and come into the land which I shall show thee.—Acts 7:2, 3.

Look unto the rock whence ye are hewn, and to the hole of the pit whence ye are digged. Look unto Abraham your father.—Isaiah 51:1, 2.

In the grey dawn of history the first great character that arrests our attention at any length is that of Abraham; who would command our notice for this, if for nothing else, that he is spoken of as the "Friend of God." Surely it must be well worthy of our devout consideration to study the inner life, and outward carriage, of such a man: that we too, in our smaller measure, may become—not servants only, but—"friends"; the favoured confidants of God—from whom He will not hide His secrets, to whom He will make known His will.

Many rays of interest focus in the story of Abraham. His portrait is drawn with such detail, that it lives before us, with the same hopes and fears, golden hours and hours of depression, that are familiar factors in our own lives. Then, also, his life is so constantly referred to in the Old Testament, and in the New, that it would seem as if the right understanding of it is necessary to give us the clue to many a difficult passage, and many a sacred doctrine, in the succeeding pages of the Bible. Nor can it fail to interest us to discover the reason why the wild Bedouin of the desert and the modern Englishman—the conservative East, and the progressive and swift-moving West; the Mohammedan and the Christian—can find in the tent of the first Hebrew a common meeting ground, and in himself a common origin.

Our story takes us back two thousand years before the

birth of Christ, and to the ancient city of Ur. And it may be well, by the aid of modern discovery, to consider the earliest conditions amid which this life was cradled. We like to stand in that lone spot among the hills, where, amid the bracken and the gorse, or from some moss-grown basin of rock, there springs forth the river which drains a continent, and flows, laden with navies to the sea. We ask the biographer to tell us something of the scenes amid which a great life was nurtured; because we think that we can better understand its colour, current, and drift. So would we thank modern discovery for having cast its lantern on the ruins of that old world city, which was the busy home of life when flocks browsed on the seven hills of Rome; and red deer, light of foot, roamed over the site of St Paul's, or came down to drink the undefiled and pellucid waters of the Thames.

We must look for Ur, not in Upper Mesopotamia, where a mistaken tradition has fixed it, but in the ruins of Mugheir, in the near vicinity of the Persian Gulf. Forty centuries, slowly silting up the shore, have driven the sea back about a hundred miles. But at the time of which we speak it is probable[1] that Abraham's natal city stood upon the coast near the spot where the Euphrates poured the volume of its waters into the ocean waves.

"The present remains of the town consist of a series of low mounds disposed in an oval shape, measuring about two miles in extent, and commanded by a larger mound of seventy feet in height, on which are the remains of what must have been once a vast temple, dedicated to the Moon."[2] In olden days it was a large and flourishing city, standing on the sea, and possessed of fleets of vessels, which coasted along the shores of the Indian Ocean, freighted with the products of the rich and fertile soil.

It would be foreign to our purpose to attempt a description of the luxuriance of that Chaldaean land, watered by its two mighty streams,[3] and in which the corn crop was of marvellous abundance, and the date-palm attained to an extraordinary growth, repaying richly the scanty labours of the people; and where pomegranates and apples, grapes and tamarisks grew wild. Suffice it to say, that it was a long green strip of garden-land, sufficient to attract and maintain vast populations of men, and specially suitable for the settlement of those shepherd-tribes which required extensive pasture lands for their herds and flocks.

These sons of Ham were grossly *idolatrous*. In that clear transparent atmosphere, the heavenly bodies blazed with extraordinary effulgence, beguiling the early Chaldaeans

8

into a system of Nature-worship, which speedily became identified with rites of gross indulgence and impurity, such as those into which humanity always falls, when it refuses to retain God in its knowledge, and gives itself up to the dictates of its own carnal lusts. The race seemed verging again on the brink of those horrible and unnatural crimes which had already necessitated its almost total destruction; and it was evident that some expedient must be speedily adopted to arrest the progress of moral defilement, and to save mankind. This enterprise was undertaken by Him, whose delights have ever been with the sons of men, and who, in after-days, could say, with majestic emphasis, 'Before Abraham was, I AM." And He accomplished His purpose then, as so often since, by *separating* to Himself one man, that through him and his descendants, when they had been thoroughly purified and prepared, He might operate upon the fallen race of man, recalling it to Himself and elevating it by a moral lever, working on a pivot outside itself.

Four centuries had passed away since the Flood; and they must have been centuries abounding in emigrations. Population multiplied more rapidly than now, and all the world was open where to choose. Leaving the first seats of life, swarm after swarm must have hived off in every direction. Surging waves of men, pressed on by hunger, love of conquest, or stronger hordes behind, spread outwards over the world. The sons of Japeth pushed northwards, to colonize Europe and Asia, and to lay the foundations of the great Indo-European family. The sons of Ham pushed southwards, over the fertile plains of Chaldaea, where, under the lead of the mighty Nimrod, they built towns of baked clay; reared temples, of which the ruins remain to this day; and cultivated the arts of civilized life to an extent unknown elsewhere. They are said to have been proficient in mathematics and astonomy; in weaving, metal-working, and gem-engraving; and to have preserved their thoughts by writing on clay tablets.

Now, it so happened, that into the midst of this Hamite colonization there had come a family of the sons of Shem. This clan, under the lead of Terah, had settled down on the rich pasture lands outside Ur. The walled cities, and civilized arts, and merchant traffic, had little attraction for them; as they were rather a race of shepherds, living in tents, or in villages of slightly-constructed huts. And if Noah's prediction were verified (Gen. 9:26), we may believe that their religious life was sweeter and purer than that of the people amongst whom we find them.

9

But, alas! the moral virus soon began its work. The close association of this Shemite family with the idolatrous and abominable practices of the children of Ham, tainted the purity and simplicity of its early faith; and it is certain that a levelling-down process was subtly at work, lowering its standard to that of its neighbours. Joshua (Joshua 24:15) says distinctly that the fathers of the children of Israel, who dwelt beyond the flood of the Euphrates, served other gods. And there are traces of the evil in the home of Laban, from which Rachel stole the images (*teraphim*), the loss of which so kindled her father's wrath (Gen. 31:19–35). It is a heavy responsibility for godly people to live amid scenes of notorious godlessness and sin. If they escape the snare, their children may be caught in it. What right have we heedlessly to expose young lives to foul miasma, which may taint and defile them for evermore! And if through the claims of duty we are compelled to live in any such baleful and noxious atmosphere, let us ask that the fire of Divine purity may extend like a cordon of defence around our home; and that our dear ones may dwell in the secret place of the Most High.

Amid such scenes ABRAHAM was born, and grew from youth to manhood. But, from the first, if we may credit the traditions which have lingered in the common talk of the unchanging East, he must have possessed no ordinary character. According to those stories, which, if not literally true, are no doubt based on a substratum of fact, as a young man Abraham offered an uncompromising opposition to the evil practices which were rife, not only in the land, but in his father's house. He employed the weapon of sarcasm, used so effectively afterwards by the prophets to his own descendants. He broke the helpless images to pieces. He refused to bow before the subtle element of fire at the bidding of the monarch, and under the penalty of martyrdom. Thus early was he being detached from the quarry of heathendom, dug from "the hole of the pit," preparatory to being shaped as a pillar in the house of the Lord.

There is nothing of all this in Scripture, but there is nothing inconsistent with it. On the contrary, as the peculiar movements of a planet suggest the presence of some celestial body of a definite size, which is yet hidden from view in the depths of space: so the mature character, the faith, and the ready obedience of this man, when he first comes under our notice, convince us that there must have been a long previous period of severe trial and testing. The mushroom is the child of a single night; but the oak, which is a match for the tempest, is the result of long years of sun and air, of breeze and storm.

At last, THE GOD OF GLORY APPEARED UNTO HIM. The light had been growing on his vision; and finally the sun broke out from the obscuring clouds. In what form of glory Jehovah revealed Himself we cannot guess; but we must believe that there was some outward manifestation which dated an epoch in Abraham's life, and gave him unmistakable basis of belief for all his future. Probably the Son, who from all eternity has been the Word of God, arrayed Himself, as afterwards on the plains of Mamre, in an angel-form; or spoke to him, as afterwards to Isaiah, from the midst of the burning seraphim (Isa. 6). In any case, the celestial vision was accompanied by a call, like that which in all ages of the world has come to loyal hearts, summoning them to awake to their true destiny, and take their place in the regeneration of the world: "Get thee out of thy country, and from thy kindred, and from thy father's house, unto the land that I will show thee" (Gen. 12:1). If we live up to our light, we shall have more light. If we are faithful in a very little, we may have the opportunity of being faithful in much. If we are steadfast in Chaldaea, we may be called out to play a great part in the history of the world. God's choice is never arbitrary; but is based on some previous traits in those whom He summons from amongst their fellows to His aid. "Whom He foreknew, He also did predestinate."

It is impossible to tell into whose hands these words may fall. Young men amid the godless tea-planters of India, or in the wild bush-life of Australia. Sailors on ship-board, and soldiers in camp. Lonely confessors of Christ in worldly and vicious societies; where there is everything to weaken, and nothing to reinforce the resistance of the brave but faltering spirit. Let all such take heart! They are treading a well-worn path, on which the noblest of mankind have preceded them; and which was much more difficult in days when few were found in it, and specially in that day, when a solitary man, the "father of many nations," trod it.

One symptom of being on that path is *loneliness*. "I called him alone" (Isa. 51:2). It was a loneliness that pressed hard on the heart of Jesus. But it is a loneliness which is assured of the Divine companionship (see John 8:16, 29; 16:32). And though no eye seems to notice the struggles and protests, and endeavours of the solitary spirit, they are watched with the sympathy of all heaven; and presently there will be heard a call, like that which started

Abraham as a pilgrim, and opened before him the way into marvellous blessedness.

Despair not for the future of the world. Out of its heart will yet come those who shall lift it up to a new level. Sauls are being trained in the bosom of the Sanhedrin; Luthers in the cloisters of the Papal Church; Abrahams under the shadows of great heathen temples, God knows where to find them. And, when the times are darkest, they shall lead forth a host of pilgrim spirits, numberless as the sand on the sea-shore; or as the star-dust, lying thick through the illimitable expanse of space.

NOTES

[1] The site of Ur is still a matter of discussion, into which I have no desire to enter. I have adopted the more recent suggestion because the distance from Charran seems to comport better with the narrative. The old site assigned to Ur was only a day or two's march from Charran, and surely Terah would not have broken up his home for so short a journey.

[2] Professor Rawlinson.

[3] The Euphrates and the Tigris.

2

The Divine Summons

*"Get thee out of thy country, and from thy
kindred, and from thy father's house, unto
the land that I will show thee: and I will
make of thee a great nation, and I will bless
thee, and make thy name great; and thou shalt
be a blessing.'—Genesis 12:1, 2.*

Whilst Abraham was living quietly in Ur, protesting against
the idolatry of his times, with all its attendant evils, and
according to tradition, suffering bitter persecution for conscience sake, "The God of glory appeared unto him, and
said, Get thee out of thy country, and from thy kindred,
and come into the land which I shall show thee (Acts
7:2, 3).

This was the first of those marvellous appearances which
anticipated the Incarnation; and marked the successive
stages of God's manifestation of Himself to men.

When this Divine appearance came we do not know;
it may have been in the still and solemn night, or in the
evening hour of meditation; or amid the duties of his
position: but suddenly there shone from heaven a great
light round about him, and a visible form appeared in the
heart of the glory, and a voice spake the message of heaven
in his ear. Not thus does God now appear to us; and
yet it is certain that He still speaks in the silence of the
waiting spirit, impressing His will, and saying, "Get thee
out." Listen for that voice in the inner shrine of thine heart.

This same voice has often spoken since. It called Elijah
from Thisbe, and Amos from Tekoa; Peter from his fishing
nets, and Matthew from his toll-booth; Cromwell from his
farm in Huntingdon, and Luther from his cloister at Erfurt.
It ever sounds the perpetual summons of God, "Come out
from her, My people, that ye be not partakers of her sins,
and that ye receive not of her plagues"; "Come out from
among them, and be ye separate, saith the Lord, and touch
not the unclean thing." Has it not come to you? Strange,
if it has not. Yet, if it has, let nothing hinder your obed-

ience; strike your tents, and follow where the God of glory beckons; and in that word COME, understand that He is moving on in front, and that if you would have His companionship, you must follow.

(1) THIS CALL INVOLVED HARDSHIP.—He was a childless man. He had sufficient for the supply of his needs. He was deeply attached to those who were united to him by the close ties of a common nature. It was no small matter for him to break up his camp, to tear himself from his nearest and dearest, and to start for a land which, as yet, he did not know.

And so must it always be. The summons of God will ever involve a wrench from much that nature holds dear. We must be prepared to take up our cross daily if we would follow where He points the way. Each step of real advance in the Divine life will involve an altar on which some dear fragment of the self-life has been offered; or a cairn beneath which some cherished idol has been buried.

It is true that the blessedness which awaits us will more than compensate us for the sacrifices which we may have to make. And the prospect of the future may well allure us forward; but still, when it comes to the point, there is certain anguish as the last link is broken, the last farewell said, and the last look taken of the receding home of past happy years. And this is God's winnowing-fan, which clearly separates chaff and wheat. Many cannot endure a test so severe and searching in its demands. Like Pliable, they get out of the slough by the side nearest to their home. Like the young man, they go away sorrowful from the One to whom they had come with haste. Shall this be the case with you? Will you hear the call of God and shrink back from its cost? Count the cost clearly indeed; but, having done so, go forward in the name and by the strength of Him in whom all things are possible and easy and safe. And in doing so you will approve yourself worthy to stand with Christ in the regeneration.

Nothing is more clear than that, in these critical days, God is summoning the whole Church to a great advance, not only in knowledge, and in spiritual experience, but also in the evangelization of the world. Blessed are they who are privileged to have a share in this sublime campaign!

(2) BUT THIS CALL WAS EMINENTLY WISE.—It was wise for *Abraham himself*. Nothing strengthens us so much as isolation and transplantation. Let a young man emigrate, or be put into a responsible position; let him be thrown

on his own resources—and he will develop powers of which there would have been no trace, if he had always lived at home, dependent on others, and surrounded by luxury. Under the wholesome demand his soul will put forth all her native vigour.

But what is true of the natural qualities of the soul is pre-eminently true of faith. So long as we are quietly at rest amid favourable and undisturbed surroundings, faith sleeps as an undeveloped sinew within us; a thread, a germ, an idea. But when we are pushed out from all these surroundings, with nothing but God to look to, then faith grows suddenly into a cable, a monarch oak, a master-principle of the life.

As long as the bird lingers by the nest, it will not know the luxury of flight. As long as the trembling boy holds to the bank, or toes the bottom, he will not learn the ecstasy of battling with the ocean wave. As long as men cling to the material, they cannot appreciate the reality of the promises of God. Abram could never have become Abraham, the father of the faithful, the mighty exemplar of faith, if he had always lived in Ur. No; he must quit his happy home, and journey forth into the untried and unknown, that faith may rise up to all its glorious proportions in his soul.

It may not be necessary for us to withdraw from home and friends; but we shall have to withdraw our heart's deepest dependence from all earthly props and supports, if ever we are to learn what it is to trust simply and absolutely on the eternal God. It may be that He is breaking away just now the shores on which we have been leaning, that the ship may glide down upon the ocean wave.

It was wise *for the world's sake*. On this one man rested the hope for the future of the world. Had he remained in Ur, it is impossible to say whether he would have continued true; or whether he might not have been seriously infected by the idolatry around. Or, even if he had been enabled to resist the adverse influences, his family, and, above all, his children, might have failed beneath the terrible ordeal. Was it not, therefore, wise for the world's sake, and for the sake of the Divine purposes, that he should be taken right away from his home and early associations, to find a fresh religious starting-point for the race, on new soil, and under new conditions?

Was it not thus that, in days of abounding vice and superstition, God led the Pilgrim Fathers to cross the seas, and found a new world, on the inhospitable shores of New England? And has it not been the plan of the

Divine government in all ages? It is impossible to move our times, so long as we live beneath their spell; but when once we have risen up, and gone, at the call of God, outside their pale, we are able to react on them with an irresistible power. Archimedes vaunted that he could lift the world, if only he could obtain, outside of it, a pivot on which to rest his lever. Do not be surprised then, if God calls you out to be a people to Himself, that by you He may react with blessed power on the great world of men.

Sometimes, indeed, He bids us stay where we are, to glorify Him there. But oftenest He bids us leave unhallowed companionships, irreligious associations, evil fellowships and partnerships, and at great cost to get ourselves away into the isolation of a land which He promises to reveal.

(3) THIS CALL WAS ACCOMPANIED BY A PROMISE.—God's commands are not always accompanied by reasons, but always by promises, expressed or understood. To give reasons would excite discussion; but to give a promise shows that the reason, though hidden, is all-sufficient. We can understand the promise, though the reason might baffle and confuse us. The reason is intellectual, metaphysical, spiritual; but a promise is practical, positive, literal. As a shell encloses a kernel, so do the Divine commands hide promises in their heart. If this is the command: "Believe on the Lord Jesus Christ"; this is the promise: "And thou shalt be saved." If this be the command: "Sell that though hast and give to the poor"; this is the promise: "Thou shalt have treasure in heaven." If this is the command: "Leave father and mother, houses and lands"; this is the promise: "Thou shalt have a hundredfold here, and everlasting life beyond." If this is the command: "Be ye separate"; this is the promise: "I will receive you and be a Father to you." So in this case: Though thou art childless, I will make of thee a great nation: though thou art the youngest son, I will bless thee, and make thy name great: though thou art to be torn from thine own family, in thee shall all the families of the earth be blessed. And each of those promises have been literally fulfilled.

It may seem that the hardships involved in the summons to exile are too great to be borne; yet study well the promise which is attached. And as the "City which hath foundations" looms on the view, it will dwarf the proportions of the Ur in which you have been content to spend your days; and you will rise to be gone. Sometimes, therefore, it seems easier not to dwell on the sacrifice involved, but on the contents of the Divine and gracious promise.

Bid people take; and they will give up of themselves. Let men find in Jesus the living water, and, like the woman of Samaria, they will leave their water-pots. Fire the hearts of the young with all the beauty and blessedness of the service of Jesus; and they will not find it so hard to leave nets, and fishing boats, and friends, to forsake all and follow Him. "When it pleased God to reveal His Son in me... immediately I conferred not with flesh and blood."

St. Francis de Sales used to say, "When the house is on fire, men are ready to throw everything out of the window; and when the heart is full of God's true love, men are sure to count all else but worthless."

(4) THIS CALL TEACHES US THE MEANING OF ELECTION.— Everywhere we find beings and things more loftily endowed than others of the same kind. This is markedly evident in the religious sphere. And there is at first a jarring wonder at the apparent inequality of the Divine arrangements; until we understand that the superior endowment of the few is intended to enable them the better to help and bless the rest. "I will bless thee, and thou shalt be a blessing."

A great thinker feels that his end is approaching; he has made grand discoveries, but he has not as yet given them to the world. He selects one of his most promising pupils, and carefully indoctrinates him with his system; he is very severe on any inaccuracies and mistakes; he is very careful to give line on line. Why does he take all this care? For the sake of the young man? Not exclusively for the pupil's benefit; but that he may be able to give to the world those thoughts which his dying master has confided to his care. The young disciple is blessed that he may pass the blessings on to others.

Is not this a glimpse into the intention of God, in selecting Abraham, and in him the whole family of Israel? It was not so much with a view to their personal salvation, though that was included; but that they might pass on the holy teachings and oracles with which they were entrusted. It would have been worse than useless to have given such jewels directly to mankind. As well put a gorgeous banquet before a hungry babe. To say the least, there was no language ready in which to enshrine the sacred thoughts of God. The genius of truth required that the minds of men should be prepared to apprehend its sacred lessons. It was needful that definitions and methods of expression should be first well learnt by the people, who, when they had learnt them, might become the teachers of mankind.

The deep question is, whether election has not much

17

more to do with our ministry than with our personal salvation. It brings less of rest, and peace, and joy, than it does of anguish, bitterness, and sorrow of heart. There is no need to envy God's elect ones. They are the exiles, the cross-bearers, the martyrs amongst men; but careless of themselves, they are all the while learning God's deepest lessons, away from the ordinary haunts of men; and they return to them presently with discoveries that pass all human thought, and are invaluable for human life.

(5) THIS CALL GIVES THE KEY TO ABRAHAM'S LIFE.—It rang a clarion note at the very outset, which continued to vibrate through all his after-history. The key to Abraham's life is the word "Separation." He was from first to last a SEPARATED MAN. Separated from his fatherland and kinsfolk; separated from Lot; separated, as a pilgrim and stranger, from the people of the land; separated from his own methods of securing a fulfilment of the promises of God; separated from the rest of mankind by special sorrows, which brought him into closer fellowship with God than has ever been reached by man; separated to high and lofty fellowship in thoughts and plans, which God could not hide from him. But it was the separation of faith. There is a form of separation known amongst men, in which the lonely soul goes apart, to secure uninterrupted leisure for devotion; spending the slow-passing hours in vigil, fasting, and prayer; hoping to win salvation as the guerdon of its austerities. This is not the separation to which God called Abraham, or to which we are summoned.

Abraham's separation is not like that of those who wish to be saved; but rather that of those who are saved. Not towards the Cross, but from it. Not to merit anything, but, because the heart has seen the Vision of God, and cannot now content itself with the things that once fascinated and entranced it; so that leaving them behind, it reaches out its hands in eager longing for eternal realities, and thus is led gradually and insensibly out and away from the seen to the unseen, and from temporal to the eternal.

May such separation be ours! May we catch the Divine Call, irradiated by the Divine Promise! And as we hear of that fair land, of that glorious city, of those Divine delights which await us, may we leave and relinquish those lesser and injurious things which have held us too long, spoiling our peace, and sapping our power; and, striking our tents, obey our God's behest, though it may lead us whither we know not!

3

"He Obeyed"

"By faith Abraham, when he was called to go out into a place which he should after receive for an inheritance, obeyed."—Hebrews 11: 8.

Ah, how much there is in those two words! Blessedness in heart, and home, and life; fulfilled promises; mighty opportunities of good—lie along the narrow, thorn-set path of obedience to the word and will of God. If Abraham had permanently refused obedience to the voice that summoned him to sally forth on his long and lonely pilgrimage, he would have sunk back into the obscurity of an unknown grave in the land of Ur, like many an Eastern sheikh before and since. So does the phosphorescent wave flash for a moment in the wake of the vessel ploughing her way by night through the southern seas; and then it is lost to sight for ever. But, thank God, Abraham obeyed, and in that act laid the foundation-stone of the noble structure of his life.

It may be that some will read these words whose lives have been a disappointment, and a sad surprise; like some young fruit tree, laden in spring with blossom, but which, in the golden autumn stands barren and alone amid the abundant fruitage of the orchard. You have not done what you expected to do. You have not fulfilled the prognostications of your friends. You have failed to realize the early promise of your life. And may not the reason lie in this, that away back in your life, there rang out a command which summoned you to an act of self-sacrifice from which you shrank? And *that* has been your one fatal mistake. The worm at the root of the gourd. The little rot within the timber. The false step, which deflected the lifecourse from the King's highway into a blind alley.

Would it not be well to ascertain if this be not so, and to hasten back to fulfil even now the long-delayed obedience, supposing it to be possible? Oh, do not think that it is now too late to repair the error of the past; or that the Almighty God will now refuse, on account of your delay, that to which He once summoned you in the young, glad years, which have taken their flight for ever. "He is merciful and gracious, slow to anger, and plenteous in goodness and truth." Do not use your long delay as an argument for longer delay, but as a reason for immediate action. "Why tarriest thou?"

Abraham, as the story shows, at first met the call of God with a mingled and partial obedience; and then for long years neglected it entirely. But the door stood still open for him to enter, and that gracious Hand still beckoned him; until he struck his tents, and started to cross the mighty desert with all that owned his sway. It was a partial failure, which is pregnant with invaluable lessons for ourselves.

(1) AT FIRST, THEN, ABRAHAM'S OBEDIENCE WAS ONLY PARTIAL.—*He took Terah with him*; indeed, it is said that "Terah took Abram his son, and Lot the son of Haran, and Sarai his daughter-in-law; and they went forth with them from Ur of the Chaldees" (Gen. 11:31). How Terah was induced to leave the land of his choice, and the graves of his dead, where his son Haran slept, we cannot tell. Was Abraham his favourite son, from whom he could not part? Was he dissatisfied with his camping grounds? Or, had he been brought to desire an opportunity of renouncing his idols, and beginning a better life amid healthier surroundings? We do not know. This, at least, is clear, that he was not whole-hearted; nor were his motives unmixed; and his presence in the march had the disastrous effect of slackening Abraham's pace, and of interposing a parenthesis of years in an obedience which, at first, promised so well. Days which break in sunlight are not always bright throughout; mists, born of earth, ascend and veil the sky: but eventually the sun breaks out again, and, for the remaining hours of daylight, shines in a sky unflecked with cloud. It was so with Abraham.

The clan marched leisurely along the valley of the Euphrates, finding abundance of pasture in its broad alluvial plains, until at last Haran was reached; the point from which caravans for Canaan leave the Euphrates to strike off across the desert. There they halted, and there they stayed till Terah died. Was it that the old man was too weary for further journeyings? Did he like Haran too well to leave it? Did heart and flesh fail, as he looked out on that far expanse of level sand, behind which the sun set in lurid glory every night? In any case, he would go no farther on the pilgrimage, and probably for as many as fifteen years, Abraham's obedience was stayed; and for that period there were no further commands, no additional promises, no hallowed communings between God and His child.

It becomes us to be very careful as to whom we take with us in our pilgrimage. We may make a fair start from our Ur; but if we take Terah with us, we shall not go far. Take care, young pilgrim to eternity, to whom you mate yourself in the marriage-bond. Beware, man of business, lest you find your Terah in the man with whom you are entering into partnership. Let us all beware of that fatal spirit of compromise, which tempts us to tarry where beloved ones bid us to stay. "Do not go to extremes," they cry; "we are willing to accompany you on your pilgrimages, if you will only go as far as Haran! Why think of going farther on a fool's errand—and whither you do not know?" Ah! this is hard to bear, harder far than outward opposition. Weakness and infirmity appeal to our feelings against our better judgment. The plains of Capua do for warriors what the arms of Rome failed to accomplish. And, tempted by the bewitching allurements, which hold out to us their syren attractions, we imitate the sailors of Ulysses, and vow we will go no farther in quest of our distant goal.

"When his father was dead, He removed him into this land" (Acts 7. 4). Death had to interpose, to set him free from the deadly incubus which held him fast. Terah must die ere Abraham will resume the forsaken path. Here we may get a solution for mysteries in God's dealings with us, which have long puzzled us; and understand why our hopes have withered, our schemes have miscarried, our income has dwindled, our children have turned against us. All these things were hindering our true development; and, out of mercy to our best interests, God has been compelled to take the knife in hand, and set us at liberty. He loves us so much that He dares to bear the pain of inflicting pain. And thus Death opens the door to Life, and through the grave we pass into the glad world of Hope and Promise which lies upon its farther side.

> "Glory to God, 'to God,' he saith.
> Knowledge by suffering entereth,
> And life is perfected through death."

(2) ABRAHAM'S OBEDIENCE WAS RENDERED POSSIBLE BY HIS FAITH.—"So Abram departed, as the Lord had spoken unto him. And he took Sarai his wife, and Lot, his

brother's son, and all their substance that they had gathered, and the souls that they had gotten in Haran, and they went forth" (Gen. 12:5). No easy matter that! It was bitter to leave the kinsfolk that had gathered around him; for Nahor seems to have followed his old father and brother up the valley to their new settlement at Haran, and we find his family living there afterwards.[1] There was no overcrowding in those ample pastures. And to crown the whole, the pilgrim actually did not know his destination, as he proposed to turn his back on the Euphrates, and his face towards the great desert. Do you not suppose that Nahor would make this the one subject of his attack?

"What do you want more, my brother, which you cannot have here?"

"I want nothing but to do the will of God, wherever it may lead me."

"Look at the dangers: you cannot cross the desert, or go into a new country without arousing the jealousy of some, and the cupidity of others. You would be no match for a troop of robbers, or an army of freebooters."

"But He who bids me go must take all the responsibility of that upon Himself. He will care for us."

"Tell me, only, whither you are going, and where you propose to settle."

"That is a question I cannot answer; for indeed, you know as much about it as I do myself. But I am sure that if I take one day's march at a time, that will be made clear—and the next and the next—until at last I am able to settle in the country which God has selected for me somewhere."

This surely was the spirit of many a conversation that must have taken place on the eve of that memorable departure. And the equivalents to our words, "Enthusiast," "Fanatic," "Fool," would be freely passed from mouth to mouth. But Abraham would quietly answer: "God has spoken; God has promised; God will do better for me than ever He has said." At night, as he walked to and fro beneath the stars, he may have sometimes been inclined to give up in despair; but then that sure promise came back again on his memory, and he braced himself to obey. "BY FAITH Abraham, when he was called to go out into a place which he should after receive for an inheritance, *obeyed*" (Heb. 11:8). Whither he went, he knew not; it was enough for him to know that he went with God. He leant not so much upon the promise as upon the Promiser: he looked not on the difficulties of his lot—but on the King eternal, immortal, invisible, the

22

only wise God; who had deigned to appoint his course, and would certainly vindicate Himself.

And so the caravan started forth. The camels, heavily laden, attended by their drivers. The vast flocks mingling their bleatings with their drovers' cries. The demonstrative sorrow of Eastern women mingling with the grave farewells of the men. The forebodings in many hearts of imminent danger and prospective disaster. Sarah may even have been broken down with bitter regrets. But Abraham faltered not. He staggered not through unbelief. He "knew whom he had believed, and was persuaded that He was able to keep that which he had committed to Him against that day." "He was fully persuaded that what God had promised, He was able to perform."

Moreover, the sacred writer tells us that already some glimpses of the "city which hath foundations," and of the "better country, the heavenly," had loomed upon his vision; and that fair vision had loosened his hold upon much which otherwise would have fascinated and fastened him.

Ah, glorious faith! this is thy work, these are thy possibilities!—contentment to sail with sealed orders, because of unwavering confidence in the love and wisdom of the Lord High Admiral: willinghood to arise up, leave all, and follow Christ, because of the glad assurance that earth's best cannot bear comparison with heaven's least.

(3) ABRAHAM'S OBEDIENCE WAS FINALLY VERY COMPLETE.—
"They went forth to go into the land of Canaan, *and into the land of Canaan they came*" (Gen. 12:5). For many days after leaving Haran, the eye would sweep a vast monotonous waste, broken by the scantiest vegetation; the camels treading the soft sand beneath their spreading, spongy feet; and the flocks finding but scanty nutriment on the coarse, sparse grass.

At one point only would the travellers arrest their course. In the oasis, where Damascus stands to-day, it stood then, furnishing a welcome resting-place to weary travellers over the waste. A village near Damascus is still called by the patriarch's name. And Josephus tells us that in his time a suburb of Damascus was called "the habitation of Abraham". And there is surely a trace of his slight sojourn there in the name of his favourite and most trusted servant, Eliezer of Damascus, of whom we shall read anon.

But Abraham would not stay here. The luxuriance and beauty of the place were very attractive; but he could not feel that it was God's choice for him. And, therefore,

ere long he was again on the southern track, to reach
Canaan as soon as he could. Our one aim in life must
ever be to follow the will of God, and to walk in those
ways in the which He has pre-ordained for us to walk.
Many a Damascus oasis, where ice-cold waters descending
from mountain ranges spread through the fevered air a
delicious coolness, and temper the scorching heat by
abundant verdure, tempts us to tarry. Many a Peter, well-
meaning but mistaken, lays his hand on us, saying, "This
shall not be unto thee: spare thyself." Many a conspirator
within the heart counsels a general mutiny against the
lonely, desolate will. And it is well when the pilgrim of
eternity refuses to stay short, in any particular, of perfect
consecration and obedience to the extreme demands of
God. When you go forth to go into the land of Canaan,
do not rest until into the land of Canaan you come.
Anything short of complete obedience nullifies all that has
been done. The Lord Jesus must have all or none; and His
demands must be fulfilled up to the hilt. But they are
not grievous.

What a glorious testimony was that which our Master
uttered when He said, "The Father hath not left Me
alone; for I do always those things that please Him."
Would that it might be true of each of us! Let us henceforth give to Christ our prompt and unlimited obedience;
sure that, even if He bids us ride into the valley of death,
it is through no blunder or mistake, but out of some sheer
necessity, which forbids Him to treat us otherwise, and
which He will ere long satisfactorily explain.

> *"Ours not to make reply,*
> *Ours not to reason why,*
> *Ours but to do and die."*

NOTE

[1] Compare Gen. 11. 29; 22. 20–3; 24. 10; 27. 43.

4

The First of the Pilgrim Fathers

Genesis 12:4-9
"Abraham departed" (Verse 4).
"Abraham went forth (Verse 5).
"Abraham passed through" (Verse 6).
"Abraham removed" (Verse 8).
"Abraham journeyed" (Verse 9).
"He went out, not knowing whither he went".
Hebrews 9:8.

All through the history of mankind there has been a little band of men, in a sacred and unbroken succession, who have confessed that they were pilgrims and strangers upon earth. Not more certainly does the scallop-shell on the monument of the cathedral aisle indicate that he whose dust lies beneath once went on pilgrimage beyond the seas, than do certain indications, not difficult to note, betray the pilgrims of the Unseen and Eternal. Sometimes they are found afar from the haunts of men, wandering in deserts and in mountains, dwelling in the dens and caves of the earth—to which they have been driven by those who had no sympathy with their other-worldliness, and hated to have so strong a light thrown on their own absorption in the concerns of the earth, and time, and sense. But very often they are to be found in the market-places and homes of men, distinguished only by their simpler dress; their girded loins; their restrained and abstemious appetite; their loose hold on gold; their independence of the maxims and opinions and applause of the world around; and the far-away look which now and again gleams in their eyes, the certain evidence of affections centred, not on the transitory things of time and earth, but on those eternal realitities which, lying beneath the veil of the visible, are only revealed to faith.

These are the pilgrims. For them the annoyances and trials of life are not so crushing or so difficult to bear; because such things as these cannot touch their true treasure, or affect their real interest. For them the royalties and glories; the honours and rewards; the delights and indulgences of men—have no attraction. They are children of a sublimer realm, members of a greater commonwealth, burgesses of a nobler city than any upon which the sun has ever looked. Foreigners may mulct an Englishman of all his spending money; but he can well afford to lose it, if all his capital is safely invested at home, in the Bank of England. How can a dukedom in some petty principality present attractions to the scion of an empire, who is passing hastily through the tiny territory, as fast as steam and wealth can carry him, to assume the supreme authority of a mighty monarchy? The pilgrim has no other desire than to pass quickly over the appointed route to his home—a track well trodden through all ages—fulfilling the duties, meeting the claims, and discharging faithfully the responsibilities devolving upon him, but ever remembering that here he has no continuing city, and seeks one which is to come.

The immortal dreamer, who has told the story of the pilgrims in words which the world will never let die, gives three marks of their appearance:

First: "They were clothed with such kind of raiment as was diverse from the raiment of any that traded in that fair. The people, therefore, of the fair made a great gazing upon them; some said they were fools, some they were Bedlams; and some they were outlandish men."

Secondly: "Few could understand what they said, they naturally spoke the language of Canaan: but they that kept the fair were the men of this world; so that from one end of the fair to the other they seemed barbarians to each other."

Thirdly: "But that which did not a little amuse the merchandizers was, that these pilgrims set very light by all their wares; they cared not so much as to look upon them, and if they called on them to buy, they would put their fingers in their ears, and cry, *Turn away mine eyes from beholding vanity,* and look upwards, signifying that their trade and traffic was in heaven."

Evidently this type of man was well known when that great dreamer dreamt—and long before. For the Apostle Peter wrote to scattered strangers (1 Pet. 1:1), and reminded them *as strangers and pilgrims,* to abstain from fleshly lusts. And long before that day, in the sunniest period of Jewish prosperity, David, in the name of his people, confessed that they were *strangers and sojourners as were all their fathers;* and that their days on earth were as a shadow on the hills, now covering long leagues of land-scape, and then hasting away, chased by glints of brilliant sun.

We left the patriarch moving leisurely southward; and thus he continued to journey forward through the land of promise, making no permanent halt, till he reached the place of Sichem, or Schechem, in the very heart of the land, where our Lord in after-years sat weary by the well. There was no city or settlement there then. The country was sparsely populated. The only thing that marked the site was a venerable oak, whose spreading arms in later ages were to shadow the excesses of a shameful idolatry.[1] Beneath this oak on the plain of Sichem, the camp was pitched; and there, at last, the long silence was broken, which had lasted since the first summons was spoken in Chaldaea, "And the Lord appeared unto Abram, and said, Unto thy seed will I give this land: and there builded he an altar unto the Lord, who appeared unto him" (Gen. 12:7).

He did not, however, stay there permanently, but moved a little to the south, to a place between Bethel and Ai; where, according to Dr. Robinson, there is now a high and beautiful plain, presenting one of the finest tracts of pasturage in the whole country.

Three things can engage our thought: the Tent, the Altar, and the Promise.

(1) THE TENT.—When Abraham left Haran his age was seventy-five. When he died he was one hundred and seventy-five years old. And he spent that intervening century moving to and fro, dwelling in a frail and flimsy tent, probably of dark camel's hair, like that of the Bedouin of the present day. And that tent was only a befitting symbol of the spirit of his life.

He held himself aloof from the people of the land. He was among them, but not of them. He did not attend their tribal gatherings. He carefully guarded against inter-marriage with their children, sending to his own country to obtain a bride for his son. He would not take from the Canaanites a thread or a sandal-thong. He insisted on paying full market value for all he received. He did not stay in any permanent location, but was ever on the move. The tent which had no foundations; which could be erected and struck in half-an-hour—this was the apt symbol of his life.

Frequently may the temptation have been presented to his mind of returning to Haran, where he could settle in the town, identified with his family. Nor were opportunities to return wanting (Heb. 11:15). But he deliberately preferred the wandering life of Canaan to the settled home of Charran; and to the end he still dwelt in a tent. It was from a tent that he was carried to lie beside Sarah in Machpelah's rocky cave. And why? The question is fully answered in that majestic chapter which recounts the triumphs of faith. "Abraham dwelt in tents, because he looked for the City which hath the foundations" (Heb. 11:9, R.V.). Precisely so: and the tent-life is the natural one for those who feel that their fatherland lies beyond the stars.

It is of the utmost importance that the children of God should live this detached life as a testimony to the world. How will people believe us, when we talk about our hope, if it does not wean us from excessive devotion to the things around us? If we are quite as eager, or careworn; quite as covetous or grasping; quite as dependent on the pleasures and fascinations of this passing world—as themselves: may they not begin to question whether our profession be true on the one hand; or whether after all there be a real city yonder on the other.

We must not go on as we are. Professing Christians are too much taken up in business cares, in pleasure-seeking, in luxury, and self-indulgence. There is a slight difference between the children of the kingdom and the children of this generation. The shrewdest observer could hardly detect any in their homes, in the education of their children, in their dress, or in their methods of doing business. They eat, they drink; they buy, they sell; they plant, they build; they marry, they give in marriage—though the flood is already breaking through the crumbling barriers to sweep them all away.

Yet how is it to be altered? Shall we denounce the present practice? Shall we inveigh against the reckless worldliness of the times? This will not affect a permanent cure. Let us rather paint with glowing colours that City which John saw. Let us unfold the glories of that world to which we are bound. Let us teach that even here, the self-denying, resolute, and believing spirit may daily tread the golden pavement, and hear even the symphonies of angel harps; and surely there will come into many a life a separateness of heart and walk which shall impress men with the reality of the unseen, as no sermon could do, however learned or eloquent.

(2) THE ALTAR.—Wherever Abraham pitched his tent,

28

he built an altar. Thus the Pilgrim Fathers, on the shores of the New World, set up their altars of worship even before they reared their homes. And long after the tent was shifted, the altar stood to show where the man of God had been.

Ah, it would be a blessed token of our religious fervour if we could set up altars in every house where we pass the night, and in every locality where it might be our hap to live, setting the example of private and family prayer, which would live long after we had passed away. If we would only dare to do it, the very Canaanites would come to revere the spot where we had knelt, and would hand on the sacred tradition, stirring coming generations to kneel there also, and call upon the name of the Lord.

Let us also remember that the altar means sacrifice, whole burnt-offering, self-denial, and self-surrender. In this sense the altar and the tent must ever go together. We cannot live the detached tent-life without some amount of pain and suffering, such as the altar bespeaks. But it is out of such a life that there spring the most intense devotion, the deepest fellowship, the happiest communion.

If your private prayer has been lately hindered, it may be that you have not been living enough in the tent. The tent-life of separation is sure to produce the altar of self-denial and of heavenly fellowship. Confess that you are a stranger and a pilgrim on the earth; and you will find it pleasant and natural to call on the name of the Lord. We do not read of Abraham building an altar, so long as he dwelt in Charran; he could not have fellowship with God whilst living in open disobedience to Him; or as long as he was ensconced comfortably in a settled life. But out of the heart of the real pilgrim life there sprang longings, desires, and aspirations, which could only be satisfied by the altars which marked his progress from place to place.

But Abraham's altar was not for himself alone. At certain periods the whole clan gathered there for common worship. A motley group that, in which slaves bought in Egypt or Ur mingled with those born in the camp; in which children and parents, young and old, stood in silent awe around the altar, where the patriarch stood to offer their common sacrifice and worship. "I know Abraham," said God, "that he will command his children and his household after him" (Gen. 18:19). He, in whom all families of the earth were to be blessed, practised family religion; and in this he sets a striking example to many Christians whose homes are altar-less. Would that Christians might be stirred by the example of the patriarch to erect the family altar, and to gather around it the daily circle of their children and dependents, for the sweetening and ennobling of their family life! Many an evil thing, like the gargoyles on the cathedral towers, would be driven forth before the hallowing influence of praise and prayer.

(3) THE PROMISE.—"Unto thy seed will I give this land" (Gen. 12:7). As soon as Abraham had fully obeyed, this new promise broke upon his ear. And it is ever thus. Disobey—and you tread a pat hunlit by a single star. Obey, live up to the claims of God—and successive promises beam out from heaven to light your steps, each one richer and fuller than the one before. Hitherto God had pledged Himself only to show the land: now He bound Himself to give it. The separated pilgrim-life always obtains promises.

There was no natural probability of that promise being fulfilled. "The Canaanite was then in the land." Powerful chieftains like Mamre and Eshcol; flourishing towns like Sodom, Salem, and Hebron; the elements of civilization—all were there. The Canaanites were not wandering tribes. They had settled and taken root. They built towns, and tilled the land. They knew the use of money and writing; and administered justice in the gate. Every day built up their power, and made it more unlikely that they could ever be dispossessed by the descendants of a childless shepherd.

But God had said it; and so it came to pass. "The counsel of the Lord standeth fast for ever; the thoughts of His heart to all generations" (Ps. 33:11). I know not what promise may be over-arching your life, my reader, with its bow of hope; but this is certain, that if you fulfil its conditions, and live up to its demands, it will be literally and gloriously fulfilled. Look not at the difficulties and improbabilities that block the path, but at the might and faithfulness of the Promiser. "Heaven and earth shall pass away, but His words shall not pass away." Not one jot or tittle shall fail (Mark 13:31; Matt. 5:18; Luke 16:17). And promise after promise shall light your life, like safety lighthouses at night along a rocky coast, which pass the vessel onward, till at last the rays of the rising sun shine full on the haven where the mariner would be.

NOTE

[1] See Jud. 9. 27–46; 1 Kings 12. 25.

5

Gone down into Egypt

*"Abram went down into Egypt to sojourn
there; for the famine was grievous in the land
[of Canaan]."*—Genesis 12:10.

The path of the separated man can never be an easy one.
He must be willing to stand alone; to go outside the camp;
and to forego the aid of many of those supplies on which
other men freely draw. It is a life, therefore, which is only
possible to Faith. When Faith is strong, we dare cut ourselves adrift from the moorings which coupled us to the
shore; and launch out into the deep, depending only on the
character and word of Him at whose command we go.
But when Faith is weak, we dare not do it; and, leaving
the upland path, we herd with the men of the world, who
have their portion in this life, and who are content with
that alone. Ah, how can we say enough of His tender
mercy, who, at such times, bends over us, with infinite
compassion, waiting to lift us back into the old heroic life!

"AND THERE WAS A FAMINE IN THE LAND."—A famine?
A famine in the Land of Promise? Yes, as afterwards, so
then; the rains that usually fall in the latter part of the
year had failed; the crops had become burnt up with the
sun's heat before the harvest; and the herbage, which should
have carpeted the uplands with pasture for the flocks, was
scanty, or altogether absent. If a similar calamity were to
befall us now, we could still draw sufficient supplies for our
support from abroad. But Abraham had no such resource.
A stranger in a strange land; surrounded by suspicious and
hostile peoples; weighted with the responsibility of vast
flocks and herds—it was no trivial matter to stand face to
face with the sudden devastation of famine.

Did it prove that he had made a mistake in coming to
Canaan? Happily the promise which had lately come to
him forbade his entertaining the thought. And this may
have been one principal reason why it was given. It came,
not only as a reward for the past, but as a preparation for

the future; so that the man of God might not be tempted beyond what he was able to bear. Our Saviour has His eye on our future, and sees from afar the enemy which is gathering its forces to attack us, or is laying its plans to beguile and entrap our feet. His heart is not more careless of us than, under similar circumstances, it was of Peter, in the darkening hour of his trial, when He prayed for him that his faith might not fail, and washed his feet with an inexpressible solemnity. And thus it often happens that a time of special trial is ushered in by the shining forth of the Divine presence, and the declaration of some unprecedented promise. Happy are they who gird themselves with these Divine preparations, and so pass unhurt through circumstances which otherwise would crush them with their inevitable pressure.

How often do professing Christians adopt a hurt and injured tone in speaking of God's dealings with them! They look back upon a sunny past, and complain that it was better with them before they entered the wicket gate and commenced to tread the narrow way. Since that moment they have met with nothing but disaster. They had no famines in Ur or Charran; but now, in the Land of Promise, they are put to sore straits and are driven to their wits' end. The trader has met with bad debts, which sorely embarrass him; the capitalist has been disappointed in several of his most promising investments; the farmer has been disheartened by a succession of bad seasons. And they complain that the service of God has brought them misfortune rather than a blessing.

But is not this the point to be borne in mind on the other side?—These misfortunes would probably have come in any case; and how much less tolerable would they have been had there not been the new sweet consciousness that God had now become the refuge of the soul! Besides this, God our Father does not undertake to repay His children in the base coin of this lower world. Spiritual grace will ever be its own reward. Purity, truth, gentleness, devotion, have no equivalent in the ore drawn from the mines of Peru, nor in the pearls of the sea; but in the happy consciousness of the heart at peace with God, and rejoicing in His smile. Had God pledged Himself to give His servants an unbroken run of prosperity, how many more counterfeit Christians would there be! Well is it that He has made no such promise; though it is certainly true that "godliness has the promise of the life that now is, and of that which is to come." Do not be surprised if a famine meets you. It is no proof of your Father's anger, but is permitted to come to test you—or to root you deeper, as the whirlwind makes the tree grapple its roots deeper into the soil.

"AND ABRAM WENT DOWN INTO EGYPT TO SOJOURN THERE."— What a marvellous history is that of Egypt, linking successive centuries. Full of mystery, wonder, and deep thinking on the destiny of man. The land of Pyramid and Sphinx, and mighty dynasties, and of the glorious Nile. We need not wonder that Egypt has ever been one of the granaries of the world, when we recall the periodic inundation of that marvellous river, which preserves the long narrow strip of green between far-reaching wastes of sand. Thither in all ages all countries have come, as Joseph's brethren did, to buy corn. The ship in which the Apostle Paul was conveyed to Rome was a corn ship of Alexandria, bearing a freight of wheat for the consumption of Rome.

In the figurative language of Scripture, Egypt stands for alliance with the world, and dependence on an arm of flesh. "Woe to them that go down to Egypt for help; and stay on horses; and trust in chariots because they are many; and in horsemen because they are very strong; but they look not unto the Holy One of Israel, neither seek the Lord!" (Isa. 31:1.)

There were occasions in Jewish story when God Himself bade His servants seek a temporary asylum in Egypt. Whilst Jacob was halting in indecision on the confines of Canaan, longing to go to Joseph, and yet reluctant to repeat the mistakes of the past, Jehovah said, "I am God, the God of thy father: fear not to go down into Egypt; for I will there make of thee a great nation: I will go down with thee into Egypt" (Gen. 46:3, 4). And, in later days, the angel of the Lord appeared to Joseph in a dream, saying, "Arise, and take the young child and his mother, and flee into Egypt" (Matt. 2:13). There may be times in all our lives when God may clearly indicate that it is His will for us to go out into the world, with a view of accomplishing some Divine purpose with respect to it. "Go, shine as lights," He seems to say. "Arrest corruption, even as salt does. Witness for Me where My name is daily blasphemed." And when God sends us, by the undoubted call of His providence, He will be as sure to keep and deliver us as He did Jacob and his seed, or the Holy Child.

But it does not appear that Abraham received any such Divine direction. He acted simply on his own judgment. He looked at his difficulties. He became paralysed with fear. He grasped at the first means of deliverance which

33

suggested itself, much as a drowning man will catch at a straw. And thus, without taking counsel of his heavenly Protector, he went down into Egypt.

Ah, fatal mistake! But how many make it still. They may be true children of God: and yet, in a moment of panic, they will adopt methods of delivering themselves which, to say the least, are questionable; and sow the seeds of sorrow and disaster in after-life, to save themselves from some minor embarrassment. Christian women plunge into the marriage bond with those who are the enemies of God, in order that they may be carried through some financial difficulty. Christian merchants take ungodly partners into business for the sake of the capital they introduce. To enable them to stave off the pressure of difficulties, and to maintain their respectability, Christian people of all grades will court the help of the world. What is all this—but going down to Egypt for help?

How much better would it have been for Abraham to have thrown the responsibility back on God, and to have said, "Thou hast brought me here; and Thou must now bear the whole weight of providing for me and mine: here will I stay till I clearly know what Thou wilt have me to do." If any should read these lines who have come into positions of extreme difficulty, through following the simple path of obedience, let them not look at God through difficulties, as we see the sun shorn of splendour through a fog; but let them look at difficulties through God. Let them put God between themselves and the disasters which threaten them. Let them cast the whole responsibility upon Him. Has He not thus brought you into difficulties, that He may have an opportunity of strengthening your faith, by giving some unexampled proof of His power? Wait only on the Lord, trust also in Him: His name is Jehovah-jireh; He will provide.

SEE HOW ONE SIN LEADS TO ANOTHER.—When Abraham lost his faith, and went down into Egypt, he also lost his courage, and persuaded his wife to call herself his sister. He had heard of the licentiousness of the Egyptians, and feared that they might take his life, to get possession of Sarah; who, even at the age which she had reached, must have been possessed of very considerable charms.

There was an element of truth in the statement that Sarah was his half-sister; but it was meant as a lie; and it certainly misled the Egyptians, "for she was taken into Pharaoh's house." It was a mean and cowardly act on Abraham's part, which was utterly indefensible. It was a cruel wrong to one who had faithfully followed his fortunes for so long. And it endangered the promised seed. Yet so it happens; when we lose our faith, and are filled with panic for ourselves, we become regardless of all and every tie, and are prepared to sacrifice our nearest and dearest, if only we may escape.

The world may entreat us well (Gen. 12:16), but that will be a poor compensation for our losses. There is no altar in Egypt, no fellowship with God, no new promises; but a desolated home, and a wretched sense of wrong. When the prodigal leaves his Father's house, though he may win a brief spell of forbidden pleasure; yet he loses all that makes life worth living, and brings himself down to the level of the swine. In such a case there is no resource, save to retrace the way that we have come, to "do the first works," and like Abraham to go up out of Egypt to the place of the altar where we were "at the first" (Gen. 13:4). Abraham's failure in Egypt gives us an insight into the original nature of the patriarch, which was by no means heroic; and betrays a vein of duplicity and deceit, similar to that which has so often re-appeared in his posterity.

How thankful should we be that the Bible does not shrink from recording the story of the sins of its noblest saints! What a proof of its veracity is here, and what encouragement there is for us!—for if God was able to make His friend out of such material as this, may we not aspire to a like privilege, though we, too, have grievously violated the high calling of faith? The one thing that God requires of His saints is implicit obedience—entire surrender. Where these are present, He can still make Abrahams out of us, though, by nature, the soil of our being is prone to barrenness and weeds.

6

Separated from Lot

"Is not the whole land before thee? separate thyself, I pray thee, from me. If thou wilt take the left hand, then I will go to the right; or, if thou depart to the right hand, then I will go to the left."—Genesis 13:9.

In our last, we saw something of the original stuff of which God makes His saints. By nature Abraham was not superior to the general run of Orientals, who do not hesitate to lie, in order to gain a point or to avert a disaster. Compared with an average Englishman, Abraham would have come off a bad second. The faith which one day was to do business in the ocean waves could not swim across a tiny creek. It is hard to imagine that such a man would ever arrive at a stature of moral greatness so commanding as to overtop all his contemporaries, and look across the ages to see the day of Christ. Yet so it was. And from that thought we may take courage.

Our God does not need noble characters, as the groundwork of His masterpieces. He can raise up stones as children. He can turn thorns into fir trees, briars into myrtle trees. He can take fishermen from their nets, and publicans from their toll-booths, making them into evangelists, apostles, and martyrs. We are not much by nature —wild, bad blood may be flowing in our veins; but God will be the more magnified, if from such stones He can raise up children unto Abraham. The miracle of His grace and power will bring more conspicuous glory to His holy Name, in proportion to the unpromising character of the materials on which He works.

"Abram went up out of Egypt, he, and his wife, and all that he had, and Lot with him, into the south."

Very marvellous this! Judging as men, we might have thought that he would never recover from that sad mistake, that disastrous failure and sin. Surely he will reap as he has sown! He will never see his faithful wife again, but must bear for ever on his conscience the brand of coward treachery! Or if, indeed, she be given again to him, he will never extricate himself from the meshes into which he has thrown himself! Irritated and deceived, Pharaoh will surely find some method of avenging the wrong with which the foreigner has repaid his generous hospitality!

But no. Contrary to all human anticipation, Jehovah appears on the behalf of his most unworthy servant. In after-years the Psalmist gives us the very words, which He uttered in the heart of the king: "Touch not Mine anointed, and do My prophets no harm (Psalm 105:15). What a marvel of tenderness! God does not cast us away for one sin. "He hath not dealt with us after our sins; nor rewarded us according to our iniquities. For as the heaven is high above the earth, so great is His mercy toward them that fear Him" (Ps. 103:10, 11). And thus, notwithstanding repeated falls and shortcomings, He lovingly pursues His Divine purpose with the soul in which the "root of the matter"[1] is found, until He sets it free from its clinging evils, and lifts it into the life of faith, and power, and familiar friendship with Himself. "Rejoice not against me, O mine enemy: when I fall, I shall arise; when I sit in darkness, then the Lord shall be a light unto me" (Micah 7:8).

Warned by this Divine voice, and restrained by a power which suffered him not to do God's servant harm, Pharaoh had commanded his men concerning him: and they had "sent him away, and his wife, and all that he had." This is how it comes to pass that we find them again traversing the uplands of Southern Palestine on their way back to Bethel, unto the place where they had halted on their first entrance into Palestine. So complete was the delivering power of God, that the Egyptian monarch did not even take back the gifts which he had bestowed as a dowry for Sarah. The "sheep, and oxen, and he-asses, and men-servants, and maid-servants, and she-asses, and camels," still remained in Abraham's possession. And we are, there-fore, prepared to learn, that "Abram was very rich, in cattle, in silver, and in gold." That visit to Egypt beyond doubt laid the foundation of the immense wealth of the family in after-time; and it was out of this that the next trouble sprang. A trouble it seemed at first; but God marvellously overruled it for drawing His child yet closer to Himself, and severing the metal to a further extent from the alloy which had clung to it too long. Hitherto, we have been told repeatedly, "and Lot went with him." This record will not be made again.

37

(1) WHO WAS LOT?—The son of Abraham's dead brother, Haran. He had probably succeeded to his father's inheritance. He may have come with his uncle across the desert in the secret hope of bettering his condition; but we will hope that he was prompted by worthier motives. He seems to have been one of those men who take right steps, not because they are prompted by obedience to God, but because their friends are taking them. Around him was the inspiration of an heroic faith, the fascination of the untried and unknown; the stir of a great religious movement: and Lot was swept into the current, and resolved to go too. He was the Pliable of the earliest Pilgrim's Progress. He may have thought that he was as much in earnest as Abraham; but it was a great mistake. He was simply an echo; a dim afterglow; a chip on the bosom of a mighty current.

In every great religious movement there always has been, and always will be a number of individuals who cast in their lot with it, without knowing the power which inspires it. Beware of them! They cannot stand the stress of the life of separation to God. The mere excitement will soon die away from them; and, having no principle to take its place, they will become hindrances and disturbers of the peace. As certainly as they are harboured in the camp, or their principles are allowed within the heart, they will lower the spiritual tone; allure to worldly policy; suggest methods which would not otherwise occur to us; and draw us towards the Egypt-world.

Nothing but supreme principle can carry any one through the real, separated, and surrendered life of the child of God. If you are prompted by anything less, such as excitement, enthusiasm, fashion, contagious example—you will first be a hindrance, and end by being a failure. Examine yourselves, whether ye be in the faith. Prove your own selves. And, if you are consciously acting from a low and selfish motive, ask God to breathe into you His own pure love. Better act from an inferior motive, if only it be in the right direction; but covet earnestly the best.

(2) THE NECESSITY OF SEPARATION.—That recent failure in connnection with Egypt may have been due, to a larger extent than we know, to the baneful influence of Lot. Had Abraham been left to himself, he might never have thought of going down to Egypt: and, in that case, there would have been another paragraph or passage in the Bible describing the exploits of faith which dared to stand to God's promise, though threatened by disaster, and hemmed

in by famine; waiting until God should bid it move, or make it possible to stay. There is something about that visit to Egypt which savours of the spirit of Lot's after-life. In any case, the time had come, in the providence of God, when this lower and more worldly spirit must go its way; leaving Abraham to stand alone, without prop, or adviser, or ally; thrown back on the counsel and help of God alone.

The outward separation of the body from the world of the ungodly is incomplete, unless accompanied and supplemented by the inner separation of the spirit. It is not enough to leave Ur, Haran, and Egypt. We must be rid of Lot also. Though we lived in a monastery, shut away from the homes and haunts of men, with no sound to break upon the ear but the summoning bell of worship, and the solemn chant; yet so long as there was an alien principle in our breast, a Lot in our heart-life, there could not be that separation to God which is the condition of the growth of faith, and of all those higher forms of the true life which make earth most like heaven. Lot must go. "Know that the Lord hath set apart him that is godly for Himself" (Ps. 4:3). No other foot then must intrude within the enclosure of the Divine proprietorship.

O souls that sigh for saintliness as harts pant for water-brooks, have ye counted the cost? Can ye bear the fiery ordeal? The manufacture of saints is no child's play. The block has to be entirely separated from the mountain bed, ere the Divine chisel can begin to fashion it. The gold must be plunged into the cleansing fire, ere it can be moulded or hammered into an ornament of beauty for the King.

As Abraham was separated from one after another of nature's resources, so must it be with all aspirants for the inner chambers of the palace of God. We must be prepared to die to to the world with its censure or praise; to the flesh, with its ambitions and schemes; to the delights of a friendship which is insidiously lowering the temperature of the spirit; to the self-life, in all its myriad subtle and overt manifestations; and even, if it be God's will, to the joys and consolations of religion.

All this is impossible to us of ourselves. But if we will surrender ourselves to God, willing that He should work in and for us that which we cannot do for ourselves, we shall find that He will gradually and effectually, and as tenderly as possible, begin to disentwine the clinging tendrils of the poisoning weed, and bring us into heart-union with Himself.

It may be that Abraham had already felt for himself the ill effect of association with Lot, and may have longed to be free from him, without knowing how the emancipation could be effected. In any case, somewhat akin to this may be the condition of some who shall read these words. Entangled in an alliance which you seem powerless to break off, your only hope is to bear it quietly till God sets you at liberty. Meanwhile guard your will, by God's grace, from swinging round, as a boat with the tide. Declare to God continually your eager desire to be emancipated. By prayer and faith get honey out of the lion's carcase. Wait patiently till God's hour strikes, and His hand opens the fast-locked door, and bids you be free. That time will come at length; for God has a destiny in store for you, so great that neither He nor you can allow it to be forfeited for any light or trivial obstacle.

(3) HOW THE SEPARATION WAS BROUGHT ABOUT.—The valleys around Bethel, which had been quite adequate for their needs when first they came to Canaan, were now altogether insufficient. The herdsmen were always wrangling for the first use of the wells, and the first crop of the pastures. The cattle were continually getting mixed. "The land was not able to bear them, that they might dwell together."

Quarrels between servants have a habit of travelling upwards, and embroiling their masters. And so Abraham and Lot would be told by their head-men of what was happening; and each would be tempted to feel irritated with the other.

Abraham saw at once that such a state of things must not be allowed to go on: especially as "the Canaanite and the Perizzite dwelt then in the land." For if those warlike neighbours heard of the dissensions in the camp, they would take an early opportunity of falling upon it. United they stood; divided, they must fall. Besides, there was the scandal of the thing, which might work prejudicially on the name and worship of that God to whom Abraham was known to bow the knee. Would that the near presence of the world might have the same wholesome effect of checking dissension and dispute among the children of the same Father!

And so Abraham called Lot to him, and said, "Let there be no strife between me and thee, and between my herdmen and thy herdmen: for we be brethren. Is not the whole land before thee? Separate thyself, I pray thee, from me. If thou wilt take the left hand, then I will go to the right;

or if thou depart to the right hand, then I will go to the left" (Gen. 13:8, 9).

The proposal was very *wise*. He saw that there was a cause for the disturbance, which would lead to similar troubles continually. If he spoke sharply to Lot, Lot would answer in the same spirit, and a breach would be made at once. So he went to the root of the matter, and proposed their separation.

His line of action was very MAGNANIMOUS. As the elder and the leader of the expedition, he had undoubted right to the first choice. But he waived his right in the interests of reconciliation.

But, above all, it was BASED ON FAITH. His faith was beginning to realize its true position; and, like a fledgling, to spread its wings for further and still further flights. Had not God pledged Himself to take care of him, and to give him an inheritance? There was no fear, therefore, that Lot could ever rob him of that which was guaranteed to him by the faithfulness of God. And he preferred, a thousand times over, that God should choose for him, than that he should choose for himself.

The man who is sure of God can afford to hold very lightly the things of this world. God Himself is his inalienable heritage; and, in having God, he has all. And, as we shall see, the man who "hedges" for himself does not do so well in the long run as the man who, having the right of choice, hands it back to God, saying: "Let others choose for themselves, if they please; but as for myself, Thou shalt choose mine inheritance for me."

> *"Not mine—not mine the choice*
> *In things or great or small;*
> *Be Thou my Guide, my Guard, my Strength,*
> *My Wisdom and my 'All'."*

NOTE

[1] Job 19. 28.

7

The Two Paths

"Is not the whole land before thee? Separate thyself, I pray thee, from me."—Genesis 13:9.

Abraham and Lot stood together on the heights of Bethel. The Land of Promise spread out before them as a map. On three sides at least there was not much to attract a shepherd's gaze. The eye wandered over the outlines of the hills which hid from view the fertile valleys nestling within their embrace. There was, however, an exception in this monotony of hill, towards the south-east, where the waters of the Jordan spread out in a broad valley, before they entered the Sea of the Plain.

Even from the distance the two men could discern the rich luxuriance, which may have recalled to them traditions of the garden once planted by the Lord God in Eden, and have reminded them of scenes which they had lately visited together in the valley of the Nile. This specially struck the eye of Lot; eager to do the best for himself, and determined to make the fullest use of the opportunity which the unexpected magnanimity of his uncle had thrown in his way. Did he count his relative a fool for surrendering the right of choice? Did he vow that he must allow no false feelings of delicacy to interfere with his doing what he could for himself? Did he feel strong in the keenness of his sight, and the quickness of his judgment? Perhaps so. For he had little sympathy with the pilgrim spirit.

But the time would come when he would bitterly rue his choice, and owe everything to the man of whom he was now prepared to take advantage.

"Lot lifted up his eyes, and beheld all the plain of Jordan, that it was well-watered everywhere...as the garden of the Lord.... Then Lot chose him all the plain of Jordan" (Gen. 13:10, 11). He did not ask what God had chosen for him. He did not consider the prejudicial effect which the morals of the place might exert upon his children and himself. His choice was entirely determined by the lust of the flesh, the lust of the eyes, and the pride of life.

For the men of Sodom were "sinners before the Lord exceedingly."

How many have stood upon those Bethel heights, intent on the same errand as took Lot thither! Age after age has poured forth its crowds of young hearts, to stand upon an exceeding high mountain, whilst before them have been spread all the kingdoms of this world, and the glory of them; the tempter whispering, that for one act of obeisance all shall be theirs. In assurance and self-confidence; eager to do the very best for themselves; prepared to consider the moralities only in so far as these did not interfere with what they held to be the main chance of life—thus have succeeding generations looked towards the plains of Sodom from afar. And, alas! like Lot, they have tried to make stones into bread; they have cast themselves down from the mountain side, for angels to catch; they have knelt before the tempter, to find his promise broken, the vision of power an illusion, and the soul beggared for ever—whilst the tempter, with hollow laugh, has disappeared, leaving his dupe standing alone in the midst of a desolate wilderness.

Let us not condemn Lot too much because he chose without reference to the moral and religious conditions of the case; lest, in judging him, we pronounce sentence on ourselves. Lot did nothing more than is done by scores of professing Christians every day.

A Christian man asks you to go over and see the place which he is about to take in the country. It is certainly a charming place: the house is spacious and well-situated; the air balmy; the garden and paddock large; the views enchanting. When you have gone over it, you ask how he will fare on Sunday. You put the question not from feelings of curiosity, but because you know that he needs strong religious influences to counteract the effect of absorbing business cares, from Monday morning till Saturday night; and because you know that his children are beginning to evince a deepening interest in the things of God. "Well," says he, "I really have never thought of it." Or perhaps he answers, "I believe there is nothing here like we have been accustomed to; but one cannot have everything: and they say that the society here is extremely good." Is not this the spirit of Lot, who bartered the altar of Abraham's camp for the plains of Sodom, because the grass looks green and plentiful?

Have mothers, professing Christians, never gone into society where evangelical religion is held in contempt, for no other reason than to make a good match for their daughters, so far, at least, as the world is concerned? Ah, the world is full of breaking hearts and wrecked happiness, because so many persist in lifting up their eyes to choose for themselves, and with sole reference to the most sordid considerations.

If Abraham had remonstrated with Lot, suggesting the mistake he was making, do you not suppose that he would have answered petulantly: "Do you not think that we are as eager as you are to serve the Lord? Sodom needs just that witness which we shall be able to give. Is it not befitting that the light should shine in the darkness; and that the salt should be scattered where there is putrefaction?" Abraham might not be able to contest these assertions, and yet he would have an inner conviction that these were not the considerations which were determining his nephew's choice. Of course, if God sends a man to Sodom, He will keep him there; as Daniel was kept in Babylon: and nothing shall by any means hurt him. He shall be kept as the eye is kept: guarded in its bony socket from violence, and by its delicate veil of eyelid sheltered from the dust. But if God does not clearly send you to Sodom, it is a blunder, a crime, a peril to go.

Mark how Lot was swiftly swept into the vortex; first he saw; then he chose; then he separated himself from Abraham; then he journeyed east; then he pitched his tent toward Sodom; then he dwelt there; then he became an alderman of the place, and sat in the gate. His daughters married two of the men of Sodom; and they probably ranked among the most genteel and influential families of the neighbourhood. But his power of witness-bearing was gone. Or if he lifted up his voice in protest against deeds of shameless vice, he was laughed at for his pains, or threatened with violence. His righteous soul might vex itself; but it met with no sympathy. He was carried captive by Chedorlaomer. His property was destroyed in the overthrow of the cities. His wife was turned into a pillar of salt. And the blight of Sodom left but too evident a brand upon his daughters. Wretched, indeed, must have been the last days of that hapless man, cowering in a cave, stripped of everything, face to face with the results of his own shameful sin.

It is, indeed, a terrible picture; and yet some such retribution is in store for every one whose choice of home, and friends, and surroundings, is dictated by the lust of worldly gain, or fashion, or pleasure, rather than by the will of God. If such are saved at all, they will be saved as Lot was —so as by fire. Now, let us turn to a more inviting theme, and further consider the dealings of the Almighty God with Abraham, the one man who was being educated to hold fellowship with Jehovah as a friend.

(1) GOD ALWAYS COMES NEAR TO HIS SEPARATED ONES.— "And the Lord said unto Abram, *after that Lot was separated from him.*" It may be that Abraham was feeling very lonely. Lot and he had been constant and close companions; and when the last of the camp-followers had moved off, and Lot had disappeared into the long distance, a cold chill may have enveloped him, as a November fog does the man who has arisen before the dawn to see his friend away by the early mail. Then it was that God spake to him.

We all dread to be separated from companions and friends. It is hard to see them stand aloof, and drop away one by one; and to be compelled to take a course by oneself. The young girl finds it hard to refuse the evening at the theatre, and to stay alone at home when her gay companions have gone off in high spirits. The young city clerk finds it hard to refuse to join in the "sweepstake," which is being got up on the occasion of some annual race. The merchant finds it hard to withdraw from the club or society with which he has long been identified, because there are practices creeping in which his conscience refuses to sanction. The Christian teacher finds it hard to adopt a course which isolates him from brethren with whom he has had sweet fellowship, but against whose views he is obliged to protest.

And yet, if we really wish to be only for God, it is inevitable that there should be many a link snapped; many a companionship forsaken; many a habit and conventionalism dropped: just as a savage must gradually and necessarily abjure most of his past, ere he can be admitted into the society and friendship of his European teacher.

But let us not stand looking on this aspect of it—the dark side of the cloud. Let us rather catch a glimpse of the other side, illuminated by the rainbow promise of God. And let this be understood, that, when once the spirit has dared to take up that life of consecration to the will of God to which we are called, there break upon it visions, voices, comfortable words, of which the heart could have formed no previous idea. For brass He brings gold, and for iron silver, and for wood brass, and for stone iron. Violence is no more heard, nor wasting, nor destruction. The sun is no more needed for the day, nor the moon for the night. Because the Lord has become the everlasting light

45

of the surrendered and separate heart, and the days of its mourning have passed away for ever.

"Come out from among them, and be ye separate, saith the Lord, and touch not the unclean thing: and I will receive you, and will be a Father unto you; and ye shall be My sons and daughters, saith the Lord Almighty. Having, therefore, these promises, dearly beloved, let us cleanse ourselves from all filthiness of the flesh and spirit" (2 Cor. 6:7).

(2) GOD WILL DO BETTER FOR THOSE WHO TRUST HIM THAN THEY COULD DO FOR THEMSELVES.—Twice here in the context we meet the phrase—"lifting up the eyes." But how great the contrast! Lot lifted up his eyes, at the dictate of worldly prudence, to spy out his own advantage. Abraham lifted up his eyes, not to discern what would best make for his material interests, but to behold what God had prepared for him. How much better it is to keep the eye steadfastly fastened on God till He says to us!— "Lift up now thine eyes, and look from the place where thou art—northward, and southward, and eastward, and westward: for all the land which thou seest, to thee will I give it, and to thy seed for ever" (Gen. 13:14, 15).

God honours them that honour Him. He withholds "no good thing from them that walk uprightly." He "meets him that rejoices and works righteousness." If only we will go on doing what is right, giving up the best to our neighbour to avoid dispute, considering God's interests first, and our own last, expending ourselves for the coming and glory of the kingdom of heaven, we shall find that God will charge Himself with our interests. And He will do infinitely better for us than we could. Lot had to ask the men of Sodom if he might sojourn among them, and he had no hold on the land; but it was all given unasked to Abraham, including that verdant circle on which Lot had set his heart. "Blessed are the meek, for they shall inherit the earth."

It is difficult to read these glowing words, *northward, and southward, and eastward, and westward,* without being reminded of "the length, and breadth, and depth, and height, of the love of Christ, that passeth knowledge." Much of the land of Canaan was hidden behind the ramparts of the hills; but enough was seen to ravish that faithful spirit. Similarly, we may not be able to comprehend the love of God in Christ, but the higher we climb the more we behold. The upper cliffs of the separated life command the fullest view of that measureless expanse.

In some parts of the Western Highlands, the traveller's eye is delighted by the clear and sunlit waters of a loch—

an arm of the sea, running far up into the hills. But as he climbs over the heathery slopes, and catches sight of the waters of the Atlantic, bathed in the light of the setting sun, he almost forgets the fair vision which had just arrested him. Thus do growing elevation and separation of character unfold ever richer conceptions of Christ's infinite love and character.

God's promises are ever on the ascending scale. One leads up to another, fuller and more blessed than itself. In Mesopotamia, God said, "I will show thee the land." At Bethel, "This is the land." Here, "I will give thee all the land, and children innumerable as the grains of sand." And we shall find even these eclipsed. It is thus that God allures us to saintliness. Not giving anything till we have dared to act—that He may test us. Not giving everything at first—that He may not overwhelm us. And always keeping in hand an infinite reserve of blessing. Oh, the unexplored remainders of God! Who ever saw His last star?

(3) GOD BIDS US APPROPRIATE HIS GIFTS.—"Arise, walk through the land in the length of it and in the breadth of it." This surely means that God wished Abraham to feel as free in the land as if the title-deeds were actually in his hands. He was to enjoy it; to travel through it; to look upon it as his. By faith he was about to act towards it as if he were already in absolute possession.

There is a deep lesson here, as to the appropriation of faith. "Be strong and very courageous" was addressed six separate times to Joshua. "Be strong" refers to the strength of the wrists to grasp. "Be very courageous" refers to the tenacity of the ankle-joints to hold their ground. May our faith be strong in each of these particulars. Strong to lay hold, and strong to keep.

The difference between Christians consists in this. For us all there are equal stores of spiritual blessing laid up in our Lord; but some of us have learnt more constantly and fully to appropriate them. We walk through the land in its lengths and breadths. We avail ourselves of the fulness of Jesus. Not content with what He is for us in the counsel of God, our constant appeal is to Him in every moment of need.

We need not be surprised to learn that Abraham removed to Hebron (which signifies fellowship), and built there an altar to the Lord. New mercies call us to deeper fellowship with our Almighty Friend, who never leaves or forsakes His own. And, as the result of his dealings with us, let us build fresh altars, and make a new dedication of ourselves and all we have to His blessed service.

47

8

Refreshment between the Battles

"Four kings with five."—Genesis 14:9.

The strife recorded in Genesis 14 was no mere border foray. It was an expedition for chastisement and conquest. Chedorlaomer was the Attila, the Napoleon of his age. His capital city, Susa, lay across the desert, beyond the Tigris, in Elam. Years before Abraham had entered Canaan as a peaceful emigrant, this dreaded conqueror had swept southwards, subduing the towns which lay in the Jordan Valley, and thus possessing himself of the master-key to the road between Damascus and Memphis. When Lot took up his residence towards Sodom, the cities of the plain were paying tribute to this mighty monarch.

At last the men of Sodom and Gomorrah, of Admah and Zeboiim, became weary of the Elamite yoke and rebelled, and Chedorlaomer was compelled to undertake a second expedition to chastise their revolt and regain his power. Combining his own forces with those of three vassal and friendly rulers in the Euphrates Valley, which lay in his way, he swept across the desert, and fell upon the wild tribes that harboured in the mountains of Bashan and Moab. His plan was evidently to ravage the whole country contiguous to those Jordan towns before actually investing them.

At last the allied forces concentrated in the neighbourhood of Sodom, where they encountered fierce resistance. Encouraged by the pitchy nature of the soil, in which horsemen and chariots would move with difficulty, the townsfolk risked an engagement in the open. In spite, however, of the bitumen pits, the day went against the effeminate and dissolute men of the plain, in whose case, as in many others, social corruption proved itself the harbinger of political overthrow. The defeat of the troops was followed by the capture and sack of those wealthy towns; and all who could not escape were manacled as slaves, and carried off in the train of the victorious army.

Sated at length with their success, their attention engrossed by their rich booty and their vast host of captives, the foreign host began slowly to return along the Jordan Valley on its homeward march. "And they took Lot, Abram's brother's son, who dwelt in Sodom, and his goods, and departed." Then one of the survivors of that fatal day climbed the hills, and made for Abraham's encampment, which he may have known in earlier days, when, as one of Lot's many servants, he lived there. "And when Abram heard that his brother was taken captive, he armed his trained servants ... and divided himself against them" (Gen. 14:14, 15).

(1) HERE IS THE UNSELFISH AND SUCCESSFUL INTERPOSITION OF A SEPARATED MAN, ON THE BEHALF OF OTHERS.—Hidden in the configuration of the country, and confederate with his friends, Abraham had watched the movements of the devastators from afar. "But they had not come nigh him; only with his eyes had he beheld and seen the reward of the wicked" (Ps. 91:8). Common prudence would have urged him not to embroil himself. "Be thankful that you have escaped, and do not meddle further in the business; lest you make these mighty kings your foes."

But true separation never argues thus. Granted that the separated one is set apart for God, yet he is set apart that he may re-act more efficiently on the great world over which God yearns, and towards which He has entertained great purposes of mercy, in the election of the few. Genuine separation—an unattachedness to the things of time and sense, because of an ardent devotion to the unseen and eternal—is the result of faith, which always works by love; and this love tenderly yearns for those who are entangled in the meshes of worldliness and sin. Faith makes us independent, but not indifferent. It is enough for it to hear that its brother is taken captive; and it will arm instantly to go in pursuit.

Ah, brothers and sisters, have there never come to you the tidings that your brothers are taken captive? How, then, is it that you have not started off long ago for their deliverance? Is this separation genuine, which stands unconcernedly by while there is such need for immediate and unselfish action?

But Abraham's interposition was as *successful* as it was unselfish and prompt. The force with which he set out was a very slender one; but his raw recruits moved quickly, and thus in four or five days they overtook the self-reliant and encumbered host amid the hills where the Jordan takes its rise. Adopting the tactics of a night attack, he fell

49

suddenly on the unsuspecting host, and chased them in headlong panic, as far as the ancient city of Damascus. "And he brought back all the goods, and also brought again his brother Lot, and his goods, and the women also, and the people" (Gen. 14:16).

Is it not always so? The men who live the life of separation and devotion towards God, are they who act with most promptness and success when the time for action comes. Lot being in Sodom, could neither elevate its morals nor save it from attack. Abraham living among the hills is alone able to cope successfully with the might of the tyrant king. Oh, do not listen to those who say you must live on the level, and in the midst of worldly men, in order to elevate and save them; and advise you to go to the theatre, the ball-room, the public-house, in order to give them a higher tone. Did Lot save Sodom? Nor will a better fate than his befall any man, who, unbidden by God, settles down in the world for his own whim and pleasure. If you would lift me, you must stand above me. If Archimedes is to move the world, he must rest his lever on a point far enough outside the earth itself.

(2) THE TIME OF A GREAT SUCCESS IS OFTEN THE SIGNAL FOR A GREAT TEMPTATION.—The King of Sodom had not been amongst the prisoners. He had probably saved himself, by a timely flight to the hills, from the field of battle. When therefore he received tidings of the patriarch's gallant and successful expedition, he set out to meet and welcome him. He would ascend from the Jordan plain by one of the gorges into the hills, and would come out on the great central road, by which Abraham and his confederates were marching back to Hebron.

The two met at the King's Dale,[1] a place to become memorable as the years went on; and situated near the city of Salem, a title which was destined to develop into the word—Jerusalem. A memorable meeting that: between the representatives of two races—the one destined to grow weaker and weaker still, until it was dispossessed by the children of that very man whose sword now saved it from utter extinction.

But more memorable than the place is the record of the spiritual encounter that took place there. Grateful for Abraham's succour and deliverance, the King of Sodom proposed to him to surrender only the persons of the captives, whilst he kept all the spoils to himself and his allies.

It must have been a very tempting offer. No slight matter

for a shepherd to have the chance of appropriating all the spoils of settled townships, so large and opulent; especially when he seemed to have some claim on them.

But he would not hear of it for a moment. Indeed, he seems to have already undergone some exercise of soul on the matter, for speaking as of a past transaction, he said, "I have lift up mine hand unto the Lord, the Most High God, the Possessor of heaven and earth, that I will not take from a thread even to a shoe-lachet; and that I will not take anything that is thine, lest thou shouldst say, 'I have made Abraham rich.'" What a magnificent contempt of specious offer! What a glorious outburst of the independence of a living faith!

There is a close parallel between this suggestion of the King of Sodom and the temptation of our Lord in the wilderness, when Satan offered Him all the kingdoms of the world for one act of obeisance. And does not this temptation assail us all? Are we not all tempted to take the gilded wage of the world, which is so eager to lay us under obligation to itself, and to feel that we are in its pay and power? The world is aware that, if we will only accept its subsidies, we shall have surrendered our position of independence, and have stepped down to its level, no longer able to witness against it, shorn of the locks of our strength, and become weak as other men.

In theory it may be argued that we can turn to good account the wealth which has been ill-gotten. But practically, we shall not find it so. The wealth of Sodom will scorch the hand that handles it, and will blight every godly enterprise to which it may be put. Besides, what right have we to depend on revenues of the world, we, who are heirs to the Possessor of heaven and earth, the children of the Great King: to whom, in giving us His Son, He has also pledged to give us all things? Better a thousand times be poor, until He make us rich with the gold that has passed through His cleansing furnace. Happy they who prefer to be pensioners on the daily providence of God to being dependent on the gold of Sodom—the wages of iniquity.

(3) THE PREVENIENT GRACE OF GOD.—It may be that Abraham would not have come off so grandly in the second conflict if he had not been prepared for it by the wondrous encounter with a greater king than either we have named. After his defeat of Chedorlaomer, and before the advent of the King of Sodom, the Hebrew had met Melchizedek, the Priest-King of Salem.

We may not stay to speak now of all the interest that gathers around this sacred figure, sacred as the type of our blessed Lord. Of that more anon. We shall be satisfied to notice now that he brought bread and wine, and blessed the weary conqueror, and coined in his hearing a new name for God. For the first time God received the title, "Possessor of heaven and earth"—one which seems to have made a deep impression upon Abraham; for we find him using it in his encounter with the King of Sodom—and it was the talisman of victory. Why should he need to take aught from man, when this new revelation of God had just fallen upon his ear, and enriched his heart for ever?

Is not this the work of the Lord Jesus still? He comes to us when wearily returning from the fight. He comes to us when He knows we are on the eve of a great temptation. He not only prays for us, as for Peter; but He prepares us for the conflict. Some new revelation; some fresh glimpse into His character; some holy thought—these are given to fill the memory and heart against the advent of the foe. Oh, matchless mercy! He forewarns and forearms us. He prevents us with the blessings of His goodness.

When next we are tempted with the bribes of an ungodly world, let us recall that name for God, which, in Abraham's case, was the talisman of victory; and let us think of Him as the POSSESSOR of heaven and earth. Why should we soil our fingers with ill-gotten gains even though they seem needful for our existence, when our Father is the Owner of all that flies in the air, treads on the land, swims in the water, or lies embedded in the rocks.

We have not infrequently been made sweet and strong, or have passed through some marked spiritual experience, for no other object than to fit us for coming peril. Let us avail ourselves of such occasions, whenever they occur, and let us ever be grateful to our Lord for victualling His castles before they are attacked, and for giving us His own new name, by which we may overcome all the wiles of men and devils.

O King of loyal hearts, may we meet Thee more often on life's highway, especially when some tempter is preparing to weave around us the meshes of evil; and bending beneath Thy blessing, may we be prepared by the communications of Thy grace for all that may await us in the unknown future!

NOTE

[1] 2 Sam. 18. 18.

9

Melchizedec

"This Melchizedec, King of Salem, priest of
the Most High God."—Hebrews 7:1.

Christ is here! The passage is fragrant with the ointment
of His name. Our hands drop with myrrh, and our fingers
with sweet-smelling myrrh, as we lay them upon the
handles of this lock (Cant. 5:5). Let us get aside from the
busy rush of life, and think long, deep thoughts of Him
who is the Alpha and Omega of Scripture, and of saintly
hearts. And let us draw from the unsearchable depths of
His nature, by the bucket of this mysterious record touch-
ing Melchizedec, the King of Salem.

There is a sense in which Christ was made *after the
order of Melchizedec*; but there is a deeper sense in which
Melchizedec was made *after the order of the Son of God*.
The writer to the Hebrews tells us that Melchizedec was
"made like unto the Son of God" (Heb. 7:3). Christ is the
Archetype of all; and from all eternity has had those
qualities which have made Him so much to us. It would
seem as if they could not stay to be manifested in the
fullness of the ages; they chafed for expression. From of
old His delights were with the sons of men. And so this
mysterious royal priest was constituted—reigning in his
peaceful city, amid the storm and wreckage of his times—
that there might be given amongst men some premonition,
some anticipation, of that glorious life which was already
being lived in Heaven on man's behalf, and which, in
due course, would be manifested on our world, and at that
very spot where Melchizedec lived his Christ-like life. Oh
that we, too, might be priests after the order of Melchizedec in this respect, if in no other, that we are made as
like as possible to the Son of God!

MELCHIZEDEC WAS A PRIEST.—The spiral column of smoke
climbing up into the clear air, in the fragrant morn, and at
the dewy eve, told that there was one heart at least which
was true in its allegiance to the Most High God: and

which bore up before Him the sins and sorrows of the clans that clustered near. He seems to have had that quick sympathy with the needs of his times which is the true mark of the priestly heart (Heb. 4:15). And he had acquired thereby so great an influence over his neighbours that they spontaneously acknowledged the claims of his special and unique position. Man must have a priest. His nature shrinks from contact with the All Holy. What is there in common between vileness and purity, darkness and light, ignorance and the knowledge which needs no telling? And in all ages, men have selected from among their fellows one who should represent them to God, and God to them. It is a natural instinct. And it has been met in our glorious Lord, who, while He stands for us in the presence of God, face to face with uncreated Light, ever making intercessions, at the same time is touched with the feeling of our infirmities, succours us in our temptations, and has compassion on our ignorance. Why need we travel farther afield? Why imitate Micah in setting up for ourselves a priest whom human hands have made? (see Jud. 17:10). Why permit any other to bear this sacred name, or to intrude on this holy office? None but Christ will satisfy or meet the requirements of God, or "become us" with unutterable needs (Heb. 7:26).

THIS PRIESTHOOD CAME OF GOD, AND WAS RATIFIED BY AN OATH.—The priests of the house of Levi exercised their office after "the law of carnal commandment" (Heb. 7:16). They assumed it, not because of any inherent fitness, or because specially summoned to the work by the voice of heaven, but because they had sprung from the special sacerdotal tribe. The Priesthood of Christ, on the other hand, is God's best gift to men—to thee, my reader, and to me; more necessary than spring flowers, or light, or air. Without it our souls would wander ever in a Sahara desert. "Christ glorified not Himself to be made a High Priest" (Heb. 5:5), but He was called of God to be a High Priest after the order of Melchizedec (ver. 10). And such was the solemnity of His appointment, that it was ratified by "the word of the oath." "The Lord sware and will not repent, Thou art a Priest for ever after the order of Melchizedec" (Heb. 7:21-8). Here is "strong consolation" indeed. No unfaithfulness or ingratitude can change this priesthood. The eternal God will never run back from that word and oath. "Eternity" is written upon the High Priest's brow: "for evermore" rings out, as He moves, from the chime of His Golden bells: "an unchangeable Priesthood"

54

is the law of His glorious being. Hallelujah! The heart may well sing, when, amid the fluctuation of earth's change, it touches at length the primeval rock of God's eternal purpose. He is "consecrated" Priest "for evermore."

THIS PRIESTHOOD WAS ALSO CATHOLIC.—Abraham was not yet circumcised. He was not a Jew, but a Gentile still. It was as the father of many nations that he stood and worshipped and received the benediction from Melchizedec's saintly hands. Not thus was it with the priesthood of Aaron's line. To share its benefit a man must needs become a Jew, submitting to the initial rite of Judaism. None but Jewish names shone in that breastplate. Only Jewish wants or sins were borne upon those consecrated lips. BUT CHRIST IS THE PRIEST OF MAN. He draws *all men* unto Himself. The one sufficient claim upon Him is that thou bear the nature which He has taken into irreversible union with His own—that thou art a sinner and a penitent pressed by conscious need. Then hast thou a right to Him, which cannot be disallowed. He is thy Priest—thine own; as if none other had claim on Him than thou. Tell Him all thy story, hiding nothing, extenuating, excusing nothing. All kindreds and people, and nations, and tongues, converge in Him, and are welcome; and all their myriad needs are satisfactorily met.

THIS PRIESTHOOD WAS SUPERIOR TO ALL HUMAN ORDERS OF PRIESTS.—If ever there were a priesthood which held undisputed supremacy among the priesthoods of the world, it was that of Aaron's line. It might not be so ancient as that which ministered at the shrines of Nineveh, or so learned as that which was exercised in the silent cloisters of Memphis and Thebes; but it had about it this unapproachable dignity—in that it had emanated, as a whole, from the Word of God. Yet even the Aaronic must yield obeisance to the Melchizedec Priesthood. And it did. For Levi was let in the loins of Abraham when Melchizedec met him; and he paid tithes in Abraham, and knelt in token of submission, in the person of the patriarch, beneath the blessing of this greater than himself (Heb. 7:4-10). Why then need we concern ourselves with the stars, when the sun has arisen upon us? What have we to do with any other than with this mighty Mediator, this Daysman, who towers aloft above all rivals; Himself sacrifice and Priest, who has offered a solitary sacrifice, and fulfils a unique ministry!

THIS PRIESTHOOD PARTOOK OF THE MYSTERY OF ETERNITY. —We need not suppose that this mystic being had literally no father, or mother, beginning of days, or end of life. The fact on which the inspired writer fixes is—that no information is afforded us on any of these points. There is an intention in the golden silence, as well as in the golden speech of Scripture. And these details were doubtless shrouded in obscurity, that there might be a still clearer approximation of the type to the glory of the Antitype, who abides continually. He is the Ancient of Days; the King of the Ages; the I AM. The Sun of His Being, like His Priesthood, knows nought of dawn, or decline from meridian zenith, or descent in the western sky. "He is made after the power of an endless life." "He ever liveth to make intercession." If, in the vision of Patmos, the hair of His head was white as snow, it was not the white of decay, but of incandescent fire. "He continueth ever, and hath an unchangeable priesthood." "He is the same yesterday, today, and for ever." He does for us now what He did for the world's grey fathers, and what He will do for the last sinner who shall claim his aid.

THIS PRIESTHOOD WAS ROYAL.—"Melchizedec, King of Salem, priest." Here again there is no analogy in the Levitical priesthood.

The royal and priestly offices were carefully kept apart. Uzziah was struck with the white brand of leprosy when he tried to unite them. But how marvellously they blended in the earthly life of Jesus! As Priest, He pitied, and helped, and fed men: as King, He ruled the waves. As Priest, He uttered His sublime intercessory prayer: as King, He spoke the "I will" of royal prerogative. As Priest, He touched the ear of Malchus: as the disowned King, to whom even Caesar was preferred, He was hounded to the death. As Priest, He pleaded for His murderers, and spake of Paradise to the dying thief: whilst His Kingship was attested by the proclamation affixed to his cross. As Priest, He breathed peace on His disciples: as King, He ascended to sit down upon His throne.

He was *first* "King of Righteousness," and after that also King of Salem, which is King of Peace (Heb. 7:2). Mark the order. Not first Peace at any price, or at the cost of Righteousness, but Righteousness first—the righteousness of His personal character; the righteous meeting, on our behalf, of the just demands of a Divine and holy law. And then founded on, and arising from, this solid and indestructable basis, there sprang the Temple of Peace, in which the souls of men may shelter from the shocks of time. "The work of righteousness shall be peace; and the effect of righteousness, quietness and assurance for ever. And My people shall dwell in a peaceable habitation, and in sure dwellings, and in quiet resting-places (Isa. 32:17, 18).

Ah, souls, what is your attitude towards Him? There be plenty who are willing enough to have Him as Priest, who refuse to accept Him as King. But it will not do. He must be King, or He will not be Priest. And He must be King in this order, first making thee right, then giving thee His peace that passeth all understanding. Waste not precious time in paltering, or arguing with Him; accept the situation as it is, and let thy heart be the Salem, the city of Peace, where He, the Priest-King, shall reign for ever. And none is so fit to rule as He who stooped to die. "In the midst of the throne stood a Lamb as it had been slain" (Rev. 5:6). Exactly! The throne is the befitting place for the Man who loved us to the death.

THIS PRIESTHOOD RECEIVES TITHES OF ALL.—"The patriarch Abraham gave a tenth of the spoils" (He. 7:4 R.V.). This ancient custom shames us Christians. The patriarch gave more to the representative of Christ than many of us give to Christ Himself. Come, if you have never done so before, resolve to give your Lord a tithe of your time, your income, your all. "Bring all the tithes into His storehouse." Nay, thou glorious One, we will not rest content with this; take all, for all is Thine. "Thine is the greatness, and the power, and the glory, and the victory, and the majesty: for all that is in the heaven and in the earth is Thine; Thine is the Kingdom, O Lord, and Thou art exalted as King above all. Now therefore, we thank Thee and praise Thy glorious name."

The Firmness of Abraham's Faith

> *"He staggered not at the promise of God
> through unbelief; but was strong in faith,
> giving glory to God."*—Romans 4:20.

In this chapter (Gen. 15), for the first time in Scripture, four striking phrases occur; but each of them is destined to be frequently repeated with many charming variations. We may speak then of this precious paragraph as of some upland vale where streamlets take their rise which are to flow seawards, making glad the lowland pasture lands on their way. Now, first, we meet the phrase, "the word of the Lord came." Here, first, we are told that "the Lord God is a shield." For the first time rings out the silver chime of that Divine assurance, "Fear not!" And now we first meet in human history that great, that mighty word, "believed." What higher glory is there for man than that he should reckon on the faithfulness of God? For this is the meaning of all true belief.

The "word of the Lord" came to Abraham about two distinct matters.

(1) GOD SPOKE TO ABRAHAM ABOUT HIS FEAR.—Abraham had just returned from the rout of Chedorlaomer and the confederate kings in the far north of Canaan; and there was a natural reaction from the long and unwonted strain as he settled down again into the placid and uneventful course of a shepherd's life. In this state of mind he was most susceptible to fear; as the enfeebled constitution is most susceptible to disease.

And there was good reason for fear. He had defeated Chedorlaomer, it is true; but in doing so he had made him his bitter foe. The arm of the warrior-king had been long enough to reach to Sodom; why should it not be long enough and strong enough to avenge his defeat upon that one lonely man? It could not be believed that the mighty monarch would settle down content until the memory of his disastrous defeat was wiped out with blood.

There was every reason, therefore, to expect him back again to inflict condign punishment. And, besides all this, as a night wind in a desert land, there swept now and again over the heart of Abraham a feeling of lonely desolation, of disappointment, of hope deferred. More than ten years had passed since he had entered Canaan. Three successive promises had kindled his hopes, but they seemed as far from realization as ever. Not one inch of territory! Not a sign of a child! Nothing of all that God had foretold!

It was under such circumstances that the word of the Lord came unto him, saying, "Fear not, Abram: I am thy Shield, and thy exceeding great Reward." Ah, our God does not always wait for us to come to Him; He often comes to us; He draws near to us in the low dungeon; He sends His angel to prepare for us the cruse of water and baken cakes, and on our souls break His tender assurances of comfort, more penetrating than the roar of the surge, "Be of good cheer; it is I; be not afraid."

But God does not content Himself with vague assurances. He gives us solid ground for comfort in some fresh revelation of Himself. And oftentimes the very circumstances of our need are chosen as a foil to set forth some special side of the Divine character which is peculiarly appropriate. What could have been more re-assuring at this moment to the defenceless pilgrim, with no stockade or walled city in which to shelter, but whose flocks were scattered far and wide, than to hear that God Himself was around him and his, as a vast, impenetrable, though invisible shield. "I am thy Shield."

Mankind, when once that thought was given, eagerly caught at it; and it has never been allowed to die. Again and again it rings out in prophecy and psalms, in temple anthem and from retired musings. "The Lord God is a sun and shield." "Thou art my hiding-place and my shield." "Behold, O God, our shield; and look upon the face of thine Anointed." "His truth shall be thy shield and buckler." It is a very helpful thought for some of us! We go every day into the midst of danger; men and devils strike at us; now it is the overt attack, and now the stab of the assassin; unkind insinuations, evil suggestions, taunts, gibes, threats; all these things are against us. But if we are doing God's will and trusting in God's care, ours is a charmed life, like that of the man who wears chain armour beneath his clothes. The Divine environment pours around us, rendering us impervious to attack, as the stream of electricity may surround a jewel-case with an atmosphere before which the stoutest attack of the most resolute felon is foiled. "No weapon that is formed against thee shall prosper" (Isa. 54:17). "Thou shalt not be afraid for the terror by night; nor for the arrow that flieth by day; nor for the pestilence that walketh in darkness; nor for the destruction that wasteth at noonday. A thousand shall fall at thy side, and ten thousand at thy right hand; but it shall not come nigh thee." Happy are they who have learnt the art of abiding within the inviolable protection of the eternal God, on which all arrows are blunted, all swords turned aside, all sparks of malice extinguished with the hissing sound of a torch in the briny waters of the sea.

Nor does God only defend us from without. He is the *reward* and satisfaction of the lonely heart. It was as if He asked Abraham to consider how much he had in having Himself. "Come now, my child, and think; even if thou wert never to have one foot of soil, and thy tent were to stand silent, amid the merry laughter of childish voices all around—yet thou wouldest not have left thy land in vain, for thou hast Me. Am not I enough? I fill heaven and earth; cannot I fill one lonely soul? Am not I 'thy exceeding great reward'; able to compensate thee by My friendship, to which thou art called, for any sacrifice that thou mayest have made?"

Our God who is love, and love in its purest, divinest essence, has given us much, and promised us more; but still His best and greatest gift is His own dear self; our reward, our great reward, our exceeding great reward. Hast thou naught? Is thy life bare? Have lover and friend forsaken thee? Art thou lonely and forsaken of all the companions of earlier, younger days? Well, answer this one question more, Hast thou God? For if thou hast, thou hast all love and life, all sweetness and tenderness, all that can satisfy the heart, and delight the mind. All lovely things sleep in Him, as all colours hide in the sunbeam's ray, waiting to be unravelled. To have God is to have all, though bereft of everything. To be destitute of God is to be bereft of everything, though having all.

(2) GOD SPOKE TO ABRAHAM ABOUT HIS CHILDLESSNESS.— It was night, or perhaps the night was turning towards the morning, but as yet myriads of stars—the watchfires of the angels; the choristers of the spheres; the flocks on the wide pasture lands of space—were sparkling in the heavens. The patriarch was sleeping in his tent, when God came near him in a vision; and it was under the shadow of that vision that Abraham was able to tell God all that was in his heart. We can often say things in the dark which we

dare not utter beneath the eye of day. And in that quiet watch of the night, Abraham poured out into the ear of God the bitter, bitter agony of his heart's life. He had probably long wanted to say something like this; but the opportunity had not come. But now there was no longer need for restraint; and so it all came right out into the ear of his Almighty Friend, "Behold, to me Thou hast given no seed: and, lo, one born in my house is mine heir." It was as if he said, "I promised for myself something more than this; I have conned Thy promises, and felt that they surely prognosticated a child of my own flesh and blood; but the slowly moving years have brought me no fulfilment of my hopes; and I suppose that I mistook Thee. Thou never intendest more than that my steward should inherit my name and goods. Ah, me! it is a bitter disappointment; but Thou hast done it, and it is well."

So we often mistake God, and interpret His delays as denials. What a chapter might be written of God's delays! Was not the life of Jesus full of them, from the moment when He tarried behind in the Temple, to the moment when He abode two days still in the same place where He was, instead of hurrying across the Jordan in response to the sad and agonized entreaty of the sisters whom He loved. So He delays still. It is the mystery of the art of educating human spirits to the finest temper of which they are capable. What searchings of heart; what analysing of motives; what testings of the Word of God; what upliftings of soul—searching what, or what manner of time, the Spirit of God signifies! All these are associated with those weary days of waiting, which are, nevertheless, big with spiritual destiny. But such delays are not God's final answer to the soul that trusts Him. They are but the winter before the burst of spring. "And, behold, the word of the Lord came unto him, saying, This shall not be thine heir; but thine own son shall be thine heir. Look now toward heaven, and tell the stars, if thou be able to number them. So shall thy seed be" (Gen. 15:4, 5). And from that moment the stars shone with new meaning for him, as the sacraments of Divine promise.

"AND HE BELIEVED IN THE LORD." What wonder that those words are so often quoted by inspired men in after ages; or that they lie as the foundation stone of some of the greatest arguments that have ever engaged the mind of man! (See Rom. 4:3; Gal. 3:6; James 2:23.)

HE BELIEVED BEFORE HE UNDERWENT THE JEWISH RITE OF

CIRCUMCISION.—The Apostle Paul lays special emphasis on this, as showing that they who were not Jews might equally have faith, and be numbered amongst the spiritual children of the great father of the faithful (Rom. 4:9-21; Gal. 3:7-29). The promise that he should be the heir of the world was made to him, when as yet he was only the far-travelled pilgrim; and so it is sure to all the seed, not to that only which is of the law, but to that also which is of the faith of Abraham, who is the father of us all.

HE BELIEVED IN FACE OF STRONG NATURAL IMPROBABILITIES.—Appearances were dead against such a thing as the birth of a child to that aged pair. The experience of many years said, "It cannot be." The nature and reason of the case said, "It cannot be." Any council of human friends and advisers would have instantly said, "It cannot be!" And Abraham quietly considered and weighed them all "without being weakened in faith" (Rom. 4:19, R.V.). Then he as carefully looked into the promise of God. And, rising from his consideration of the comparative weight of the one and the other, he elected to venture everything on the word of the Eternal. Nay, that was not all; as shock followed shock, and wave succeeded wave, booming with crash of thunder on his soul, he staggered not; he did not budge an inch; he did not even tremble, as sometimes the wave-beat rock shivers to its base. He reckoned on the faithfulness of God. He gave glory to God. He relied implicitly on the utter trustworthiness of the Divine veracity. He was "fully assured that what He had promised He was able also to perform." Ah, child of God, for every look at the unlikelihood of the promise, take ten looks at the promise: this is the way in which faith waxes strong. "Looking unto the promise of God, he wavered not through unbelief, but waxed strong" (Rom. 4:20, R.V.).

HIS FAITH WAS DESTINED TO BE SEVERELY TRIED.—If you take to the lapidary the stones which you have collected in your summer ramble, he will probably send the bulk of them home to you in a few days, with scanty marks of having passed through his hands. But some one or two of the number may be kept back, and when you inquire for them, he will reply: "Those stones which I returned are not worth much: there was nothing in them to warrant the expenditure of my time and skill; but with the others, the case is far otherwise: they are capable of taking a polish and of bearing a discipline which it may take months and even years to give; but their beauty, when the process is complete, will be all the compensation that can be wished."

Some men pass through life without much trial, because their natures are light and trivial, and incapable of bearing much, or of profiting by the severe discipline which, in the case of others, is all needed, and will yield a rich recompense, after it has had its perfect work. God will not let any one of us be tried beyond what we are able to bear. But when He has in hand a nature like Abraham's, which is capable of the loftiest results, we must not be surprised if the trial is long continued, almost to the last limit of endurance. The patriarch had to wait fifteen years more, making five-and-twenty years in all, between the first promise and its fulfilment in the birth of Isaac.

HIS FAITH WAS COUNTED TO HIM FOR RIGHTEOUSNESS.— Faith is the seed-germ of righteousness; and, when God sees us possessed of the seed, He counts us as also being in possession of the harvest which lies hidden in its heart. Faith is the tiny seed which contains all the rare perfumes and gorgeous hues of the Christian life, awaiting only the nurture and benediction of God. When a man believes, it is only a matter of education and time to develop that which is already in embryo within him; and God, to whom the future is already present, accounts the man of faith as dowered with the fruits of righteousness, which are to the glory and praise of God. But there is a deeper meaning still than this—in the possession through faith of a judicial righteousness in the sight of God.

The righteousness of Abraham resulted not from his works, but from his faith. "He believed God; and it was reckoned unto him for righteousness." "Now it was not written for his sake alone, that it was reckoned unto him; but for our sake also, unto whom it shall be reckoned, who believe on Him that raised Jesus our Lord from the dead" (Gal. 3:6; Rom. 4:23, 24 R.V.). Oh, miracle of grace! if we trust ever so simply in Jesus Christ our Lord, we shall be reckoned as righteous in the eye of the eternal God. We cannot realize all that is included in those marvellous words. This only is evident ,that faith unites us so absolutely to the Son of God that we are ONE with Him for evermore; and all the glory of His character —not only what he was when He became obedient unto death, but what He is in the majesty of His risen nature— is reckoned unto us.

Some teach imputed righteousness as if it were something apart from Christ, flung over the rags of the sinner. But it is truer and better to consider it as a matter of blessed identification with Him through faith; so that as He was one with us in being made sin, we are one with Him in being made the Righteousness of God. In the counsels of Eternity that which is true of the glorious Lord is accounted also true of us who, by a living faith, have become members of His body, of His flesh, and of His bones. Jesus Christ is made unto us Righteousness, and we are accepted in the Beloved. There is nothing in faith, considered in itself, which can account for this marvellous fact of imputation. Faith is only the link of union; but inasmuch as it unites us to the Son of God, it brings us into the enjoyment of all that He is as the Alpha and Omega, the Beginning and the End, the First and the Last.

II

Watching with God

(Genesis 15:7)

*"The vision is yet for an appointed time, but
at the end it shall speak, and not lie. Though
it tarry, wait for it: because it will surely
come; it will not tarry."*—Habakkuk 2:3.

*"It is good that a man should both hope
and quietly wait for the salvation of the
Lord."*—Lamentations 3:26.

*"If we hope for that we see not, then do
we with patience wait for it."*—Romans 8:25.

It is not easy to watch with God, or to wait for Him.
The orbit of His providence is so vast. The stages of His
progress are so wide apart. He holds on His way through
the ages; we tire in a few short hours. And when His
dealings with us are perplexing and mysterious, the heart
that had boasted its unwavering loyalty begins to grow
faint with misgivings, and to question—When shall we
be able to trust absolutely, and not be afraid?

In human relationships, when once the heart has found
its rest in another, it can bear the test of distance and
delay. Years may pass without a word or sigh to break
the sad monotony. Strange contradictions may baffle the
understanding and confuse the mind. Officious friends may
delight in putting unkind and false constructions on conduct confessedly hard to explain. But the trust never varies
or abates. It knows that all is well. It is content to exist
without a token, and to be quiet without attempting to
explain or defend. Ah, when shall we treat God so? When
shall we thus rest in Him, trusting where we cannot understand? Can any education be too hard which shall secure
this as its final and crowning result? Surely that were
heaven, when the heart of man could afford to wait for a
millennium, unstaggered by delay, untinged by doubt.

At this stage, at least of his education, Abraham had not
learnt this lesson. But in that grey dawn, as the stars
which symbolized his posterity were beginning to fade in

the sky, he answered the Divine assurance that he should inherit the land of which he as yet did not own a foot, by the sad complaint: "Lord God, whereby shall I know that I shall inherit it?"

How human this is! It was not that he was absolutely incredulous: but he yearned for some tangible evident token that it was to be as God had said; something he could see; something which should be an ever-present sacrament of the coming heritage, as the stars were of the future seed. Do not wonder at him; but rather adore the love which bears with these human frailties, and stoops to give them stepping-stones by which to cross the sands to the firm rock of an assured faith.

(1) WATCHING BY THE SACRIFICE.—In those early days, when a written agreement was very rare, if not quite unknown, men sought to bind one another to their word with the most solemn religious sanctions. The contracting party was required to bring certain animals, which were slaughtered and divided into pieces. These were laid on the ground in such a manner as to leave a narrow lane between; up and down which the covenanting party passed to ratify and confirm his solemn pledge.

It was to this ancient and solemn rite that Jehovah referred, when he said, "Take Me an heifer of three years old, and a she-goat of three years old, and a ram of three years old, and a turtle-dove, and a young pigeon. And he took unto him all these, and divided them in the midst, and laid each piece one against another" (Gen. 15:8, 10).

It was still the early morning. The day was young. And Abraham sat down to watch. Then there came a long pause. Hour after hour passed by; but God did not give a sign or utter a single word. Judging by appearances, there was neither voice, nor any to answer, nor any that regarded.

Higher and ever higher the sun drove his chariot up the sky, and shone with torrid heat on those pieces of flesh lying there exposed upon the sand; but still no voice or vision came. The unclean vultures, attracted by the scent of carrion, drew together as to a feast, and demanded incessant attention if they were to be kept away. Did Abraham ever permit himself to imagine that he was sitting there on a fool's mission? Did not the thought instil itself into his mind, that perhaps after all he had been led to arrange those pieces by a freak of his own fancy, and that God would not come at all? Did he shrink from the curious gaze of his servants, and of Sarah his wife, because half-conscious of having taken up a position he could not justify?

We cannot tell what passed through that much-tried heart during those long hours. But this, at least, we recognize; that this is in a line with the discipline through which we all have to pass. Hours of waiting for God! Days of watching! Nights of sleepless vigil! Looking for the outposts of the relief that tarries! Wondering why the Master comes not! Climbing the hill again and again, to return without the expected vision! Watching for some long-expected letter, till the path to the Post Office is trodden down with constant passing to and fro, and wet with many tears! But all in vain! Nay, but it is not in vain. For these long waiting hours are building up the fabric of the spirit-life, with gold, and silver, and precious stones, so as to become a thing of beauty, and a joy for evermore.

Only let us see to it that we never relax our attitude of patience, but wait to the end for the grace to be brought unto us. And let us give the unclean birds no quarter. We cannot help them sailing slowly through the air, or uttering dismal screams, or circling around us as if to pounce. But we *can* help them settling down. And this we must do, in the name and by the help of God. "If the vision tarry, wait for it."

(2) THE HORROR OF A GREAT DARKNESS.—The sun at last went down, and the swift Eastern night cast its heavy veil over the scene. Worn out with the mental conflict, the watchings, and the exertions of the day, Abraham fell into a deep sleep. And in that sleep his soul was oppressed with a dense and dreadful darkness; such as almost stifled him, and lay like a nightmare upon his heart. "Lo, a horror of great darkness fell upon him."

Do my readers understand something of the horror of that darkness? When one who has been brought up ·in a traditional belief, which fails to satisfy the instincts of maturer life, supposes that in letting go the creed, there must also be the renunciation of all faith and hope, not seeing that the form may go, whilst the essential substance may remain: when one, mistaking the nature of sin and the mercy of God, fears that there has been committed an unpardonable sin, or that the bounds of repentance have been overstepped for ever: when some terrible sorrow which seems so hard to reconcile with perfect love, crushes down upon the soul, wringing from it all its peaceful rest in the pitifulness of God, and launching it on a sea unlit by a ray of hope: when unkindness, and cruelty, and monstrous injustice browbeat, and mock, and maltreat the trusting heart, till it begins to doubt whether there be a God overhead who can see and still permit—these know something of the horror of great darkness; and what weird and frightful visions will in that darkness pass one after another before the spirit, like the phantoms of a drunkard's delirium or the apparitions of an unhealthy brain.

It was a long and dark prospect which unfolded itself before Abraham. He beheld the history of his people through coming centuries, strangers in a foreign land, enslaved and afflicted. Did he not see the anguish of their soul, and their cruel bondage beneath the task-master's whips? Did he not hear their groans, and see mothers weeping over their babes, doomed to the insatiable Nile? Did he not witness the building of Pyramid and Treasure-city, cemented by blood and suffering? It was, indeed, enough to fill him with darkness that could be felt.

And yet the sombre woof was crossed by the warp of silver threads. The enslaved were to come out, and to come out with great substance, their oppressors being overwhelmed with crushing judgment. They were to come into that land again. Whilst, as for himself, he should go to his fathers in peace, and be buried in a good old age.

It is thus that human life is made up: brightness and gloom; shadow and sun; long tracks of cloud, succeeded by brilliant glints of light. And amid all, Divine justice is working out its own schemes, affecting others equally with the individual soul which seems the subject of especial discipline. The children of Abraham must not inherit the Land of Promise till the fourth generation has passed away, because the iniquity of the Amorites had not yet filled up the measure of their doom. Only then—when the reformation of that race was impossible; when their condition had become irremediable, and their existence was a menace to the peace and purity of mankind—was the order given for their extermination, and for the transference of their power to those who might hold it more worthily.

Oh, ye who are filled with the horror of great darkness because of God's dealings with mankind, learn to trust that infallible wisdom which is co-assessor with immutable justice; and know that He who passed through the horror of the darkness of Calvary, with the cry of forsakenness, is ready to bear you company through the valley of the shadow of death, till you see the sun shining upon its further side. "Who is among you that walketh in darkness, and hath no light? Let him trust in the name of the Lord, and stay upon his God."

(3) THE RATIFICATION OF THE COVENANT.—When Abraham awoke, the sun was down. Darkness reigned supreme. "It was dark." A solemn stillness brooded over the world. Then came the awful act of ratification. For the first time since man left the gates of Eden there appeared the symbol of the glory of God; that awful light which was afterwards to shine in the pillar of cloud, and the Shekinah gleam.

In the thick darkness, that mysterious light—a lamp of fire—passed slowly and majestically between the divided pieces; and, as it did so, a voice said: "Unto thy seed have I given this land, from the river of Egypt unto the great river, the river Euphrates" (Gen. 15:18).

Remember that promise made with the most solemn sanctions, never repealed since, and never perfectly fulfilled. For a few years during the reign of Solomon the dominions of Israel almost touched these limits, but only for a very brief period. The perfect fulfilment is yet in the future. Somehow the descendants of Abraham shall yet inherit their own land, secured to them by the covenant of God. Those rivers, shall yet form their boundary lines: for "the mouth of the Lord hath spoken it."

As we turn from this scene—in which God bound Himself by such solemn sanctions, to strengthen the ground of His servant's faith—we may carry with us exalted conceptions of His great goodness, which will humble itself so low in order to secure the trust of one poor heart. By two immutable things, His word and oath, God has given strong assurance to us who are menaced by the storm, drawing us on to a rock-bound shore. Let us, by our Forerunner, send forward our anchor, Hope, within the vail that parts us from the unseen: where it will grapple in ground that will not yield, but hold until the day dawn, and we follow it into the heaven guaranteed to us by God's immutable counsel (Heb. 6:19, 20).

12

Hagar, the Slave Girl

*Now Sarai, Abram's wife, had a handmaid,
an Egyptian, whose name was Hagar.*—
Genesis 16:1.

We none of us know all that is involved when we tear ourselves from the familiar scenes of our Harans to follow
God into the lands of separation which lie beyond the
river. The separated life cannot be an easy one. We may
dimly guess this as we step out into the untried and
unknown; but God graciously veils from our eyes that
which would needlessly startle and daunt us; unfolding
to us His requirements, only as we are able to bear them.

The difficulties of the separated life arise, not from any
arbitrary appointments of Divine Providence, but from the
persistent manifestations of the self-life in its many Protean
forms. It is absurd to say that it dies once for all in some
early stage of the Christian life; and it is perilous to
lead men to think so. When men think or boast that it
is dead, it peeps out in their very assertions, and laughs
at the success of its efforts to blind them to its presence.
This is the masterpiece of its art: to cajole its dupes
into thinking that it is dead. Gangs of thieves always like
to secure the insertion of a paragraph in the newspapers,
announcing that they have left the neighbourhood, because,
in the false security which is induced by the announcement, they are more able to carry out their plans of pillage.

We say, in the first moments of consecration, that we
are eager, not only to be reckoned dead in the sight of
God, so far as our self-life is concerned, but to be dead.
And if we really mean what we say, God undertakes the
work, first of revealing the insidious presence of the self-
life where we had least expected it, and then of nailing
it in bitter suffering to the cross of a painful death. O ye
who know something of the analysis of your inner life, do
not your hearts bear witness that, as the light of heaven
breaks with glowing glory on your souls, it reveals unexpected glimpses into the insidious workings of self?—so much

so that you are driven to claim, with no bated breath: first, Divine forgiveness for harbouring such a traitor; and then, the interposition of Divine grace to mete out that death which is the only condition of growth and blessedness.

There is here a very startling manifestation of the tenacity with which Abraham's self-life still survived. We might have expected that by this time it had been extinguished: the long waiting of ten slow-moving years: the repeated promises of God: the habit of contact with God Himself—all this had surely been enough to eradicate and burn out all confidence in the flesh; all trust in the activities of the self-life; all desire to help himself to the realization of the promises of God. Surely, now, this much-tried man will wait until, in His own time and way, God shall do as He has said. Abraham would not take a shoe-latchet, or a thread, from the King of Sodom, because he was so sure that God would *give* him all the land. Nor was he disappointed: when God said, "I am thy exceeding great reward." And similarly we might have expected that he would have strenuously resisted every endeavour to induce him to realize for himself God's promise about his seed. Surely he will wait meekly and quietly for God to fulfil His own word, by means best known to Himself.

Instead of this he listened to *the reasoning of expediency,* which happened to chime in with his own thoughts, and sought to gratify the promptings of his spirit by doing something to secure the result of which God had spoken. Simple-hearted faith waits for God to unfold His purpose, sure that He will not fail. But mistrust, reacting on the self-life, leads us to take matters into our own hands—even as Saul did, when he took upon himself to offer sacrifice, without awaiting the arrival of Samuel.

(1) THE QUARTER WHENCE THESE REASONINGS CAME.— "Sarai said unto Abram." Poor Sarah! She had not had her husband's advantages. When he had been standing in fellowship with God, she had been quietly pursuing the routine of household duty, pondering many things.

It was clear that Abraham should have a son; but it was not definitely said by God that the child would be hers. Abraham was a strict monogamist; but the laxer notions of those days warranted the filling of the harem with others, who occupied an inferior rank to that of the principal wife, and whose children, according to common practice, were reckoned as if they were her own. Why should not her husband fall in with those laxer notions of the marriage vow? Why should he not marry the slave-girl, whom they had either purchased in an Egyptian slave market, or acquired amongst the other gifts with which Pharaoh had sent them away?

It was an heroic sacrifice for her to make. She was willing to forego a woman's dearest prerogative; to put another in her own place; and to surrender a position to which she had a perfect right to cling, even though it seemed to clash with the direct promise of God. But her love to Abraham; her despair of having a child of her own; and her inability to conceive of God fulfilling His word by other than natural means—all these things combined to make the proposal from which, in another aspect, her wifely nature must have shrunk. Love in Sarah did violence to love.

No one else could have approached Abraham with such a proposition, with the slightest hope of success. But when Sarah made it, the case was altered. The suggestion might have flitted across his own mind, in his weaker moments, only to be instantly rejected and put aside, as doing a grievous wrong to his faithful wife. But now, as it emanated from her, there seemed less fear of it. It was supported by the susceptibilities of natural instinct. It was consistent with the whisperings of doubt. It seemed to be a likely expedient for realizing God's promise. And without demur, or reference to God, he fell in with the proposal. "Abram hearkened to the voice of Sarai."

It is always hard to resist temptation when it appeals to natural instinct or to distrusting fear. At such an hour, if the Saviour be not our Keeper, there is small hope of our being able to resist the double assault. But the temptation is still more perilous when it is presented, not by some repellent fiend, but by some object of our love; who, like Sarah, has been the partner of our pilgrimage, and who is willing to sacrifice all in order to obtain a blessing which God has promised, but has not yet bestowed.

We should be exceedingly careful before acting on the suggestions of any who are not as advanced as we are in the Divine life. What may seem right to them may be terribly wrong for us. And we should be especially careful to criticise and weigh any proposals which harmonize completely with the tendencies of our self-life. "If the wife of thy bosom, or thy friend, which is as thine own soul, entice thee secretly...thou shalt not consent unto him, nor hearken unto him; neither shall thine eye pity him, neither shalt thou spare" (Deut. 13:6–8). But does not the response of the soul to such suggestions indicate how far the self-life is from being dead?

(2) THE SORROWS TO WHICH THEY LED.—As soon as the end was obtained, the results, like a crop of nettles, began to appear in that home, which had been the abode of purity and bliss; but which was now destined to be the scene of discord. Raised into a position of rivalry with Sarah, and expectant of giving the long-desired son to Abraham, and a young master to the camp, Hagar despised her childless mistress, and took no pains to conceal her contempt.

This was more than Sarah could endure. It was easier to make one heroic act of self-sacrifice, than to bear each day the insolent carriage of the maid whom she had herself exalted to this position. Nor was she reasonable in her irritation; instead of assuming the responsibility of having brought about the untoward event, so fraught with misery to herself, she passionately upbraided her husband, saying: "My wrong be upon thee: the Lord judge between me and thee" (Gen. 16:5).

How true this is to human nature! We take one false step, unsanctioned by God; and when we begin to discover our mistake, we give way to outbursts of wounded pride. But instead of chiding ourselves, we turn upon others, whom we may have instigated to take the wrong course, and we bitterly reproach them for wrongs of which they at most were only instruments, whilst we were the final cause.

Out of this fleshly expedient sprang many sorrows. Sorrow to Sarah, who on this occasion, as afterwards, must have drunk to the dregs the cup of bitter gall; of jealousy and wounded pride; of hate and malice, which always destroy peace and joy in the nature, from which they stream as the fiery lava torrents from a volcanic crater. Sorrow to Hagar, driven forth as an exile from the home of which she had dreamt to become the mistress, and to which she had thought herself essential. Ah, bitter disappointment! Sorrow to Abraham, loth to part with one who, to all human appearance, would now become the mother of the child who should bless his life: stung, moreover, as he was, by the unwonted bitterness of his wife's reproaches.

If any should read these words who are tempted to use any expedients of human devising for the attainment of ends, which in themselves may be quite legitimate, let them stand still, and take to heart the teachings of this narrative. For, as surely as God reigns, shall every selfish expedient involve us in unutterable and heartrending sorrow. "From this time shalt thou have wars."

73

(3) THE VICTIM WHOSE LIFE-COURSE WAS SO LARGELY INVOLVED.—We cannot be surprised at the insolent bearing of the untutored slave-girl. It was only what might have been expected. But we mourn to see in her only one of myriads who have been sacrificed to the whim or passion, to the expediency or selfishness, of men. Innocent and light-hearted, she might have been the devoted wife of some man in her own station and the mother of a happy family. But, taken as she was from her true station, and put into a position in which she was a mother without being a lawful wife, what could her lot be but misery in the home in which she had no proper status, and at last in the exiled and homeless wanderings in which Sarah's bitter jealousy twice drove her: once for a time—afterwards for ever?

Abraham, for the sake of the peace of his home, dared not interpose between his wife and her slave. "Behold," said he, "thy maid is in thy hand; do to her as it pleaseth thee." Not slow to act upon this implied consent, the irate mistress dealt so bitterly with the girl that she fled from her face, and took the road, trodden by the caravans, towards her native land.

"The angel of the Lord" (and here, for the first time, that significant expression is used, which is held by many to express some evident manifestation of the Son of God in angel-guise) "found her by a well of water" which was familiarly known in the days of Moses. There, worn, and weary, and lonely, she sat down to rest. How often does the Angel of the Lord still find us in our extremity! —when we are running away from the post which was assigned to us; when we are evading the cross. And what questions could be more pertinent, whether to Hagar or to us: "Whence camest thou? and whither wilt thou go?" Reader, answer those two questions, ere thou readest further. What is thine origin? and what thy destiny?

Then there followed the distinct command, which applies to us evermore, "Return, and submit." The day would come when God Himself would open the door, and send Hagar out of that house (chap. 21 : 12–14). But until that moment should come, after thirteen years had rolled away, she must return to the place which she had left, bearing her burden and fulfilling her duty as best she might. "Return, and submit."

We are all prone to act as Hagar did. If our lot is hard, and our cross is heavy, we start off in a fit of impatience and wounded pride. We shirk the discipline; we evade the yoke; we make our own way out of the difficulty. Ah!

we shall never get right thus. Never! We must retrace our steps; we must meekly bend our necks under the yoke. We must accept the lot which God has ordained for us, even though it be the result of the cruelty and sin of others. We shall conquer by yielding. We shall escape by returning. We shall become free by offering ourselves to be bound. "Return, and submit." By and by, when the lesson is perfectly learnt, the prison-door will open of its own accord.

Meanwhile the heart of the prodigal is cheered by promise (Gen. 16:10). The Angel of the Lord unfolds all the blessed results of obedience. And as the spirit considers these, it finds the homeward way no longer lined by flints, but soft with flowers.

Nor is this all: but in addition to promise, there breaks on the soul the conception of One who lives and sees; who lives to avenge the wronged, and to defend the helpless; and who sees each tear and pang of the afflicted soul.

"Thou art a God that seeth." Not like those blind Egyptian idols that stare with stony gaze across the desert: having eyes, though they see not. It was a new thought to the untutored slave-girl; it is familiar enough to us. And yet we might find new depths of meaning in life and duty, if every moment were spent in the habitual realization of these words. Let us look after Him that seeth us. Let us often stay the whirr of life's shuttles to say softly to ourselves, "God is here; God is near; God sees—He will provide; He will defend; He will avenge." "The eyes of the Lord run to and fro throughout the whole earth, to show Himself strong in the behalf of them whose heart is perfect toward Him" (2 Chron. 16:9; Zech. 4:10).

13

"Be Thou Perfect!"

I am the Almighty God: walk before Me, and be thou perfect.—Genesis 17:1.

Thirteen long years passed slowly on after the return of Hagar to Abraham's camp. The child Ishmael was born, and grew up in the patriarch's house—the acknowledged heir of the camp, and yet showing symptoms of the wild-ass nature of which the angel had spoken (16:12, R.V.). Not a little perplexed must Abraham have been with those strange manifestations; and yet the heart of the old man warmed to the lad, and clung to him, often asking that Ishmael might live before God.

And throughout that long period there was no fresh appearance, no new announcement. Never since God had spoken to him in Charran had there been so long a pause. And it must have been a terrible ordeal, driving him back on the promise which had been given, and searching his heart to ascertain if the cause lay within himself. Such silences have always exercised the hearts of God's saints, leading them to say with the Psalmist: "Be not silent to me; lest, if Thou be silent to me I become like them that go down into the pit" (Ps. 28:1). And yet they are to the heart what the long silence of winter is to the world of nature, in preparing it for the outburst of spring.

Some people are ever on the outlook for Divine appearances, for special manifestations, for celestial voices. If these are withheld, they are almost ready to break their hearts. And their life tends to an incessant straining after some startling evidence of the nearness and the love of God. This feverishness is unwholesome and mistaken. Such manifestations are, indeed, delightful; but they are meant as the bright surprises, and not as the rule of Christian life: they are flung into our lives as a holiday into the school routine of a child, awakening thrilling and unexpected emotions of joy. It is true that they are liable to be withheld when we are walking at a distance from God, or indulging in coldheartedness and sin. But it is not always so. And when the child of God has lost these bright visitations for long and sad intervals—if, so far as can be ascertained, there is no sense of condemnation on the heart for known unfaithfulness—then it must be believed that they are withheld, not in consequence of palpable sin, but to test the inner life, and to teach the necessity of basing it on faith, rather than on feelings however gladsome, or experiences however divine.

At last, "when Abram was ninety years old and nine," the Lord appeared unto him again, and gave him a new revelation of Himself; unfolded the terms of His covenant; and addressed to him that memorable charge, which rings its summons in the ear and heart of every believer still: "Walk before Me, and be thou perfect."

(1) THE DIVINE SUMMONS.—"Walk before Me, and be thou perfect." Men have sadly stumbled over that word. They have not erred, when they have taught that there is an experience, denoted by the phrase, which is possible to men. But they have sadly erred in pressing their own significance into the word, and in then asserting that men are expected to fulfil it, or that they have themselves attained it.

"Perfection" is often supposed to denote sinlessness of moral character, which at the best is only a negative conception, and fails to bring out the positive force of this mighty word. Surely perfection means more than—sinlessness. And if this be admitted, and the further admission be made, that it contains the thought of moral completeness then it becomes yet more absurd for any mortal to assert it of himself. The very assertion shows the lack of any such thing, and reveals but slender knowledge of the inner life and of the nature of sin. *Absolute sinlessness* is surely impossible for us so long as we have not perfect knowledge; for as our light is growing constantly, so are we constantly discovering evil in things which once we allowed without compunction: and if those who assert their sinlessness live but a few years longer, and continue to grow, they will be compelled to admit, if they are true to themselves, that there was evil in things which they now deem to be harmless. But whether they admit it or not, their shortcomings are not less sinful in the sight of the holy God, although undetected by their own fallible judgment. And as to *moral completeness*, it is enough to compare the best man whom we ever knew with the perfect beauty of God incarnate, to feel how monstrous such an assumption is. Surely the language of the Apostle Paul better becomes our lips, as he cries, "Not as though I had already attained, or were already perfect; but I follow after." Perhaps in the dateless noon of eternity such words will still best become our lips.

Besides all this, the word "perfect", bears very different renderings from those often given to it. For instance, when we are told that the man of God must be *perfect* (2 Tim. 3:17), the underlying thought, as any scholar would affirm, is that of a workman being "thoroughly equipped for his work," as when a carpenter comes to the house, bearing in his hand the bag in which all necessary tools are readily available. Again, when we join the prayer that the God of Peace would make us *perfect* in every good work to do His will, we are, in fact, asking that we may be "put in joint" with the blessed Lord; so that the glorious Head may freely secure through us the doing of His will (Heb. 13:20, 21). Again, when our Lord bids us be *perfect* as our Father in heaven is perfect, He simply incites us to that "impartiality of mercy" which knows no distinctions of evil and good, of unjust and just, but distributes its favours with bountiful and equal hand (Matt. 5:48).

What, then, is the true force and significance of this word in that stirring command which lies before us here, "Walk before Me, and be thou perfect"? A comparison of the various passages where it occurs establishes its meaning beyond a doubt, and compels us to think into it the conception of "whole-heartedness." It denotes the entire surrender of the being; and may be fairly expressed in the well-known words of the sweet and gifted songstress of modern days:

"True hearted, whole hearted, faithful and loyal,
King of our lives, by Thy grace will be."

This quality of whole-hearted devotion has ever been dear to God. It was this that He considered in Job, and loved in David. It is in favour of this that His eyes run to and fro to show Himself strong (2 Chron. 16:9). It is for this that He pleads with Abraham; and it was because He met with it to so large an extent in his character and obedience that He entered into eternal covenant bond with him and his.

Here let each reader turn from the printed page, to the record of the inner life lying open to God alone, and ask, "Is my heart perfect with God? Am I whole-hearted towards Him? Is He first in my schemes, pleasures, friendships, thoughts, and actions? Is His will my law, His love my light, His business my aim, His 'well-done!' my exceeding great reward? Do others share me with Him?"

78

There is no life to be compared with that of which the undivided heart is the centre and spring. Why not seek it now?—and, turning to God in holy reverie, ask Him to bring the whole inner realm under His government, and to hold it as His for evermore. "If thine eye be single, thy whole body shall be full of light" (Matt. 6:22).

And such an attitude can only be *maintained by a very careful walk.* "Walk before Me, and be thou perfect." We must seek to realize constantly the presence of God, becoming instantly aware when the fleeciest cloud draws its vail for a moment over His face, and asking whether the cause may not lie in some scarcely-noticed sin. We must cultivate the habit of feeling Him near, as the Friend from whom we would never be separated, in work, in prayer, in recreation, in repose. We must guard against the restlessness and impetuosity, the excessive eagerness and impatience, which drown the accents of His still, small voice. We must abjure all expedients He does not inspire, all actions He does not promote. We must often turn from the friend, the poem, the landscape, or the task, to look up into His face with a smile of loving recognition. We must constantly have the watches which we carry next to our hearts synchronized by His eternal movements. All this must be. And yet we shall not live forced or unnatural lives. None so blithe or light-hearted as we. All the circles of our daily life will move on in unbroken order and beauty; just as each shining moon circles around its planet, because the planet obeys the law of gravitation to the sun. Would you walk before God? Then let there be nothing in heart or life which you would not open to the inspection of His holy and pitiful eye.

(2) THE REVELATION ON WHICH THIS SUMMONS WAS BASED. "I am the Almighty God" ('EL-SHADDAI'). What a name is this! And what awful emotions it must have excited in the rapt heart of the listener! God had been known to him by other names, but not by this. And this was the first of a series of revelations of those depths of meaning which lay in the fathomless abyss of the Divine name, each disclosure marking an epoch in the history of the race.

In God's dealings with men you will invariably find that some transcendent revelation precedes the Divine summons to new and difficult duty; promise opens the door to precept: He gives what He commands, ere He commands what He wills. And on this principle God acted here. It was no child's play to which He called His servant. To walk always before Him—when heart was weak, and strength was frail, and the temptation strong to swerve to right or left. To be perfect in devotion and obedience, when so many crosslights distracted, and perplexed, and fascinated the soul. To forego all methods of self-help, however tempting. To be separated from all alliances that others permitted or followed. This was much. And it was only possible through the might of the Almighty. Abraham could only do all these things on the condition, on which the Apostle insisted in after-days, that God should strengthen him. And, therefore, it was that there broke on him the assurance: "I am the Almighty God." It is as if He had said: "All power is Mine in Heaven, and upon earth. Of old I laid the foundations of the earth, and the heavens are the work of My hands. I sit upon the circle of the earth; and its inhabitants are as grasshoppers. I bring out the starry hosts by number, calling them all by names, by the greatness of My might, for that I am strong in power: not one faileth. Hast thou not known—has thou not heard—that the everlasting God, the Lord, the Creator of the ends of the earth fainteth not, neither is weary?'

All this is as true to-day as ever. And if any will dare venture forth on the path of separation, cutting themselves aloof from all creature aid, and from all self-originated effort; content to walk alone with God, with no help from any but Him—such will find that all the resources of the Divine Almightiness will be placed at their disposal, and that the resources of Omnipotence must be exhausted ere their cause can fail for want of help. O children of God, why do we run to and fro for the help of man, when the power of God is within reach of the perfect heart? But this condition must be fulfilled ere that mighty power can be put in operation on our behalf. "To him that overcometh I will give a white stone, and in the stone a new name written." In Abraham's case, that name, graved on the glistening jewel, was "I am the Almighty God"; for Moses it was "Jehovah"; for us it is "the God and Father of our Lord Jesus Christ".

(3) THE COVENANT WHICH WAS DIVINELY PROPOSED.— "I will make My covenant between Me and thee." A covenant is a promise made under the most solemn sanctions, and binding the consenting parties in the most definite and impressive way. What mortal would not consent when the Almighty God proposed to enter into an everlasting covenant with His creature, ordered in all things and sure, and more stable than the everlasting hills!

It referred to the seed.—And there was a marked

advance. In Haran it ran thus, "I will make of thee a great nation." At Bethel, thus, "Thy seed shall be as the dust of the earth." At Mamre, thus, "Tell the stars; so shall thy seed be." But now, three times over, the patriarch is told that he should be the father of many nations, a phrase explained by the Apostle as including all, of every land, who share Abraham's faith, though not sprung from him in the line of natural descent (Gal. 3:7-29). In memoy of that promise his name was slightly altered, so that it signified the "father of a great multitude". "Nations of thee, and kings of thee (Gen. 17:6). *We* are included in the golden circle of those words, if we believe; and we may claim the spiritual part, at least, of this covenant, which was made with Abraham before he was circumcised.

It referred to the land.—"I will give unto thee, and to thy seed after thee, the land wherein thou art a stranger, all the land of Canaan, for an everlasting possession." This promise waits for fulfilment. The word "everlasting" must mean something more than those few centuries of broken, fitful rule. The recent immigration of Jews to Palestine may be an initial stage to its realization. But there is a time, no doubt, at hand when our covenant-keeping God will build again the tabernacle of David, which is fallen down, and will repair the ruins thereof; and the land, shall be again inhabited by the seed of Abraham His friend.

It referred to the coming child.—Till then Abraham had no other thought than that Ishmael should be his heir. But this could not be: (1) because he was slave-born; and the slave abideth not in the house for ever: (2) because he was a child of the flesh, and not the direct gift of God. Abraham had been left to wait till the hope of children had become as remote from him as it had been for years from his wife; so that the heir should be evidently the creation of the Almighty God, whose name was disclosed, ere this astounding announcement was made. This is why we are kept waiting till all human and natural hope has died from our hearts, so that God may be All in all. "And God said, Sarah thy wife shall bear thee a son indeed; and thou shalt call his name Isaac" (*ver.* 19).

For us there is yet a crowning sweetness in the words, "I will be a God unto thee, and to thy seed; words repeated, in Hebrews 8:10, so as certainly to include us all, if we believe. Who can unfold all the wealth of meaning of these words? All light, and no darkness at all. All love, and no shadow of change. All strength, and no sign of weakness. Beauty, sweetness, glory, majesty, all are in God, and all these will be thine and mine, if God saith to us, "I will be a God unto thee."

Nor shall this heritage be ours only: it shall belong to our children also, if we exercise Abraham's faith. God pledges Himself to be the God of our seed. But it is for us to claim the fulfilment of His pledge. Not in heart-rending cries, but in quiet, determined faith, let us ask Him to do as He has said.

14

The Sign of the Covenant

*I will make My covenant between Me and
thee, and will multiply thee exceedingly.—*
Genesis 17:2.

Three times over in Scripture Abraham is called "the
friend of God." In that moment of agony, when tidings
came to King Jehoshaphat of the great heathen alliance
which had been formed against him, he stood in the
Temple, and said, "Art not Thou our God, who didst
drive out the inhabitants of this land ... and gavest it to
the seed of Abraham, thy friend, for ever?" (2 Chron.
20:7).

And the Apostle James, at the close of his argument
about faith and works, tells us that when Abraham believed
God, "it was imputed unto him for righteousness, and
he was called the friend of God" (James 2:23).

But, better than all, Jehovah Himself uses the title
of friendship, and acknowledges the sacred tie between
this much tried spirit and Himself: "Thou Israel art my
servant, Jacob whom I have chosen, the seed of Abraham
My friend" (Isa. 41:8).

And it would almost appear as if these two chapters,
Genesis 17: and 18, had been written for this, among
other things: to show the familiarity and intimacy which
existed between the Eternal God and the man who was
honoured to be called His "friend". However, in reading
them, we must not suppose that there was something
altogether exceptional and unique in this marvellous story.
Without doubt it is a true record of what happened more
than three thousand years ago; but it is surely also intended
as a specimen of the way in which the Eternal God is
willing to deal with true-hearted saints in all ages. To
hundreds, and perhaps thousands, of His saints, God has
been all that He was to Abraham; and He is willing to be
all that to us still.

Let us peruse these ancient lines beneath the flood of
light shed on them by our Saviour, when He said: "Hence-

forth I call you not servants; for the servant knoweth not what his lord doeth; but I have called you friends" (John 15:15).

The friendship of God is freely offered to us in Jesus Christ our Lord. We cannot merit or deserve it. We cannot establish a prior claim to it. We are simply His bankrupt debtors for ever, wondering at the heights and depths, the lengths and breadths, of the unsearchable riches of His grace. May we not say that one ultimate cause of this friendship is in the yearning of the heart of the Eternal for fellowship? But it must remain for ever a mystery why He should seek it amongst ourselves; the fallen children of Adam; the tenants of bodies of dust; the aphidæ on the tiny leaf, called earth, amidst the forest foliage of the universe.

Surely, if He had so desired it, He might have found—or if He could not have found, He might have created—a race more noble, more obedient, more sympathetic than ourselves. Or, at least, He might have secured one which should not cost Him so dearly, demanding of Him the anguish of Gethsemane, and the blood of the cross. So, perhaps, we are sometimes prone to think. And yet it could not be. That which is, and has been, must on the whole be the best that could be, since infinite love and wisdom have so ordered it. And perhaps none could be so perfectly the companions and fellows of the Son of God through all the ages as those who know the light, because they have dwelt in the darkness; who know the truth, because they have been ensnared in the meshes of the false; and who can appreciate love, because they have been in the far country, wasting their substance in riotous living, but have been redeemed by His blood.

But what a wondrous destiny there is within our reach! One to which the first-born sons of light might aspire in vain! At the best they can only be ministers, flames of fire, hearts of love, excelling in strength, hearkening to His word. But we may be the FRIENDS of God; sons and daughters of the great King; members of the body of Christ; constituent parts of His Bride, in her peerless beauty and meetness for her Spouse. As one writes such words as these, the brain almost reels beneath the conception that flashes before it of the blessedness which awaits us, both in this world, and in those ages which rear their heads in the far distance, as lines on lines of snowy breakers rolling in from a sunlit sea.

Oh, FRIENDS OF GOD! why do you not make more of your transcendent privileges? Why do you not talk to Him about all that wearies and worries you, as freely as Abraham did, telling Him about your Ishmaels, your Lots, and His dealings? Why do you not fall on your faces while God talks with you (Gen. 17:3)? Life should be one long talk between God and us. No day at least should close without our talking over its history with our patient and loving Lord; entering into His confessional; relieving our hearts of half their sorrow, and all their bitterness, in the act of telling Him all. And if only we get low enough, and be still enough, we shall hear His accents sweet and thrilling, soft and low, opening depths which eye hath not seen, nor ear heard; but which He has prepared for those who love and wait for Him.

There are, however, three conditions to be fulfilled by us if we would enjoy this blessed friendship: SEPARATION, PURITY, and OBEDIENCE, each of which was set forth in the rite of circumcision, which was given to Abraham for himself and his descendants at this time.

Circumcision seems to have been in vogue among the Egyptians and other nations, even before it was taken up and adopted as the seal of the sacred covenant between God and Abraham. It existed previously; but it had never borne the interpretation with which it was now invested; just as the immersion of new disciples had been long practised both by the Baptist and the Jews, before our Lord appropriated it and gave it a significance which opened up in it entirely fresh depths of meaning and beauty.

We are all of us more or less dependent on outward symbols and signs; and Abraham and his children were no exception to this rule; and it therefore seemed good to God to carve in the flesh of His people an unmistakable reminder and sacrament of that holy relationship into which they had entered. A similar function, in the Christian Church, is met by the ordinances of Believers' Baptism and the Lord's Supper.

The rite of circumcision was rigorously maintained amongst the children of Abraham. Moses was not permitted to undertake his life-work whilst his son was left uncircumcised. Nor were the people allowed to enter Canaan until they had rolled away the reproach of Canaan, and had submitted to this rite on the threshold of the Land of Promise. The sanctity of the Sabbath might at any time be invaded, rather than permit the eighth day of a child's life to pass without the act of circumcision being performed. It is said of the child Jesus that "eight days were fulfilled for circumcising Him" (Luke 2:21, R.V.). Paul noted the fact that in his own life, according to Jewish usage, he was "circumcised the eighth day (Phil. 3:5). And no one could receive benefit through sin-offering or sacrifice who had not passed through this initiatory rite. So strict was the line of demarcation, that the Jew counted the uncircumcised as unclean, and would not eat with them or go into their houses. It was a formidable charge against the Apostle Peter, on his return to Jerusalem from visiting in the house of Cornelius, "Thou wentest in to men uncircumcised, and didst eat with them" (Acts 11:3).

It was concerning this matter that controversy waxed so warm in the early Church. The Pharisee party were quite willing for Gentiles to meet with them in Church fellowship, if they were circumcised as Jews; but not otherwise. They went so far as to affirm, "Except ye be circumcised after the manner of Moses ye cannot be saved" (Acts 15:1, 24). And, not content with affirming this in Antioch and Jerusalem, they sent their emissaries far and wide, especially visiting the churches which had been recently founded by the Apostle Paul's assiduous care, and insisting upon the circumcision of the new converts so soon as he had turned his back.

There was no compromise possible in this matter; and both the Council at Jerusalem and the Apostle Paul, guided by the Spirit of God, made it abundantly clear, both by circular letter and epistle, that circumcision was part of the temporary ritual of Judaism, which was destined to pass away. "If ye be circumcised, Christ shall profit you nothing." "In the new man there is neither circumcision nor uncircumcision." "In Christ Jesus neither circumcision availeth anything nor uncircumcision, but a new creature" (Gal. 5:2; Col. 3:11; Gal. 5:6; 6:15). And thus this danger was averted from the Church, which had been in peril of becoming a Jewish institution, a kind of inner circle of the Judaistic commonwealth, but which henceforth became the common meeting-ground for all who loved, trusted, and obeyed the Lord Jesus in sincerity.

At the same time, as in so many other Jewish rites, there was an inner spirit, which passed on into the Christian Church, and is our heritage to-day. St. Paul, the deadly foe of the outward rite, speaks of the spiritual circumcision, and says it is made without human hands, by the direct interposition of the Holy Spirit: and that it consists in "the putting-off of the body of the sins of the flesh" (Col. 2:11). Oh, blessed High Priest, this is what we need: take the knife in hand; and, though it cost us blood, make haste to set us free from the dominion of evil, and to constitute us the true circumcision: "For we are the circumcision, which worship God in the Spirit, and rejoice in Christ Jesus, and have no confidence in the flesh" (Phil. 3:3).

It is only in proportion as we know the spiritual meaning of circumcision that we can enter into the joyous appropriation of the friendship of God. But if we are willing, our Lord and Saviour is both able and willing to effect in us this blessed spiritual result.

(1) SEPARATION.—Abraham and his seed were marked out by this rite as a separated people. And it is only as such that any of us can be admitted into the friendship of God. Blood-shedding and death—the cross and the grave —must lie between us and our own past life; yea, between us and all complicity with evil. The only trysting place for Christ and His followers is outside the camp, where the ground is still freshly trodden by the feet of the exiled King.

There are times when we may be expressly bidden to abide where we were originally called of God; but this will be for special purposes of ministry, and because the darkness needs light, and the carcase requires salt. For the most part the clarion note rings out to all who are wishful to know the sweets of Divine fellowship: "Come out from among them, and be ye separate, saith the Lord, and touch not the unclean thing; and I will receive you, and will be a Father unto you" (2 Cor. 6:17, 18).

This was the key to Abraham's life; and is the inner meaning of the rite of circumcision.

(2) PURITY.—"Putting off the body of the flesh by the circumcision of Christ (Col. 2:11, R.V.). There is hardly a single grace dearer to God than this—to keep lily-white amid the defiling atmosphere: to walk with unspotted garments even in Sardis: to be as sensitive to the taint of impurity as the most delicate nostril to an evil odour. Ah, this is a condition of great price in the sight of God, and one to which He unveils Himself. "Blessed are the pure in heart, for they shall see God" (Matt. 5:8).

Purity can only be attained by the special grace of the Holy Spirit; and by doing two things: first, by our turning instantly from paragraphs in papers, or pictures on the walls, and all things else, which excite impure imaginations; secondly, by our seeking immediate forgiveness, when we are conscious of having yielded, even for a moment, to the deadly and insidious fascinations of the flesh.

There are some who sigh after the white rose of chastity, with a kind of despair that it should ever become their own. They forget that it is only possible to us by the grace of Christ, and through the Holy Spirit; whose temples we profess ourselves to be. Let us trust Him to keep His own property in the perfect loveliness of that purity and chastity which are so dear to God; this is the circumcision of Christ.

(3) OBEDIENCE.—For Abraham this rite might have seemed less necessary than for some in his camp. But no sooner was it commanded than it was undergone. "In the self-same day was Abraham circumcised, and Ishmael his son." Does it not remind us of Him who said, "Ye are My friends, if ye do whatsoever I command you"? Instant obedience to known duty is an indispensable condition of all intimacy with God: and if the duty be irksome and difficult, then remember to claim all the more of the Divine grace; for there is no duty, to which we are called, for the discharge of which there is not strength enough within reach, if only we will put forth our hands to take it.

We do not obey in order to become friends; but having become friends we hasten to obey. Love is more inexorable than law. And for the love of Him who calls us by so dear a title, we are glad to undertake and accomplish what Sinai with all its thunders would fail to nerve us to attempt.

Of the secrets which shall be revealed; of the delights which shall be experienced; of the blessings which shall accrue to ever widening circles, through the friendship of one man with God—we have not space to speak. This, however, is true, that the soul laughs to itself (*ver.* 17), not with incredulity, but with the uncontrollable gladness of conscious acceptance and love.

15

The Divine Guest

The Lord appeared unto Abraham in the
plains of Mamre.—Genesis 18:1.

When, in the course of some royal progress, a sovereign
deigns to sojourn in the homestead of one of the subjects
of his realm, the event becomes at once the theme of
chroniclers, and the family selected for so high an honour
is held in deepened respect. But what shall we say in
the presence of such an episode as this—in which the
God of heaven became the guest of His servant Abraham!

There is no doubt as to the august character of one of
the three who, on that memorable afternoon, when every
living thing was seeking shelter during the heat of the day,
visited the tent of the patriarch. In the first verse we
are expressly told that Jehovah appeared unto him in the
plains of Mamre, as he sat in the tent door in the heat of
the day. And in the tenth verse there is the accent of
Deity, who alone can create life, and to whom nothing is
too hard, in the words of promise which tell how certainly
Sarah should have a son. And, besides, we are told that
two angels came to Sodom at even. Evidently they were two
of the three who had sat as Abraham's guests beneath the
tree which sheltered his tent in the blazing noon. But as
for the other, who throughout the wondrous hours had
been the only spokesman, His dignity is disclosed in the
amazing colloquy which took place on the heights of
Mamre, when Abraham stood yet before the Lord, and
pleaded with Him as the Judge of all the earth.

It was thus that the Son of God anticipated His incarnation; and was found in fashion as a man before He became
flesh. He loved to come *incognito* into the homes of
those He cherished as His friends, even before He came
across the slopes of Olivet to make His home in the
favoured cottage, where His spirit rested from the din of
the great city, and girded itself for the cross and the tomb.
"He rejoiced in the habitable part of the earth, and His
delights were with the sons of men" (Prov. 8:31).

It is very marvellous! We may well ask with deepest reverence and awe the question of Solomon, when he felt the utter inadequacy of his splendid Temple as the abode of the eternal God: "Will God in very deed dwell on the earth? Behold, heaven and the heaven of heavens cannot contain Thee; how much less this house that I have builded!" (1 Kings 8:27, R.V.). But this question has been for ever settled by God Himself, in the majestic words: "Thus saith the high and lofty One that inhabiteth eternity, whose name is Holy; I dwell in the high and holy place; with him also that is of a contrite and humble spirit, to revive the spirit of the humble, and to revive the heart of the contrite ones" (Isa. 57:15). And the life of our blessed Master is a delightful commentary on these mighty affirmations. He said to a publican, "Zaccheus, make haste and come down, for today I must abide at thy house." He went to the home of Peter, and was ministered to by one of the household, whom He had raised from the gates of death. And after His resurrection, He entered the humble lodging of the two disciples in whose company He had walked from Jerusalem, seeking to dry their tears as they went.

Nor is that all. There is no heart so lowly but that He will enter. There is no home so humble, but that He will make Himself a welcome inmate. There is no table so poorly provided, but that He will sit thereat, turning water into wine, multiplying the loaves and fishes, and converting the simple meal into a sacrament. When seated at meat with those He loves, He still takes bread, and blesses it and breaks, and gives to them (Luke 24:30). To each and all He says, as He stands laden with raiment, eyesalve, gold, and viands for the evening meal: "Behold, I stand at the door, and knock: if any man hear My voice, and open the door, I will come in to him, and will sup with him; and he with Me" (Rev. 3:20).

Abraham evidently, at the outset, did not realize the full meaning of the episode in which he was taking part. Even so do we often fail to value aright characters with whom we come in contact. It is only as they pass away from us for ever, and we look back upon them, that we realize that we have been entertaining angels unawares. Let us so act always and everywhere, that as we review the past we may have nothing to regret; and may not have to reproach ourselves with having omitted to do something or other, which we would have inserted in our programme had we only realized our opportunities.

ABRAHAM TREATED HIS VISITORS WITH TRUE EASTERN HOSPITALITY.—He *ran* to meet them, and bowed himself toward the ground. He proposed water for their feet, and rest for their tired frames, beneath the spreading shadow. He started his wife to the immediate kneading of the meal for baking on the scorching stones. He ran to choose his tenderest calf, refusing to delegate the work to another's hand. He served his visitors himself, and stood as a servant by their side, under the tree, while they did eat. Christians have not much to boast of—and a good deal to learn—as they consider the action of this old-time saint, and his dealings with the three strangers who came to his tent. The faith which he had towards God had a very winsome aspect towards men. There was nothing in him which was austere or forbidding; but much that was exceedingly lovely, and brimming with the milk of human kindness.

MAY IT NOT BE THAT CHRIST COMES TO US OFTEN IN THE GUISE OF A STRANGER?—But we are too busy, or too tired, or too much afraid of making a mistake; and, therefore, we either refuse Him altogether, or we treat Him so badly that He passes unobserved away, to carry to some one else the blessing which He would have left with us had we only shown ourselves worthy.

Does He not test us thus? Of course if He were to come in His manifested splendour as the Son of the Highest, every one would receive Him, and provide Him with sumptuous hospitality. But this would not reveal our true character. And so He comes to us as a wayfaring man, hungry and athirst; or as a stranger, naked and sick. Those that are akin to Him will show Him mercy, in whatsoever disguise He comes, though they recognize Him not, and will be surprised to learn that they ever ministered to Him. Those, on the other hand, who are not really His, will fail to discern Him; will let Him go unhelped away; and will wake up to find that "inasmuch as they did it not to one of the least of these, they did it not to Him" (Mat. 25:45).

There was much truth in the simplicity of the little German lad, who left the door open for the Lord to enter and sit with his mother and himself at their frugal supper-table; and who, as a beggar stood within the portal, asking alms, remarked: "Perhaps the Lord could not come Himself, and had therefore sent this poor man as His representative."

BUT GOD NEVER LEAVES US IN HIS DEBT.—He takes care

to pay for His entertainment, royally and divinely. He uses Peter's fishing smack, and gives it back, nearly submerged by the weight of the fish which He had driven into the nets. He sits down with His friends to a country marriage-feast, and pays for their simple fare by jars brimming with water turned to wine. He uses the five barley loaves and two small fishes; but He fills the lad with an ample meal. He sends His prophet to lodge with a widow, and provides meal and oil for him and her for many days. And Abraham was no loser by his ready hospitality; for, as they sat at meat, the Lord foretold the birth of Sarah's child: "I will certainly return unto thee; and Sarah thy wife shall have a son."

Sarah was sitting inside the flimsy curtain of camel's hair, secluded after the Eastern fashion for those of high rank; and as she heard the words, she laughed within herself the laugh of incredulity. That laugh was at once noticed by Him from whom nothing can be hid, and whose eyes are as a flame of fire. "And the Lord said unto Abraham, Wherefore did Sarah laugh, saying, Shall I of a surety bear a child, which am old? Is anything too hard for the Lord?" (Gen. 18 : 13, 14).

With strange simplicity she answered through the curtain, denying that she had laughed: for she was afraid. But her reply was met by the stern and uncompromising asseveration, which was altogether final, "Nay, but thou didst laugh." These were the only audible words which we know to have passed between God and Abraham's wife; and they reveal the superficiality and unbelief of her nature. But we must not judge her too harshly, for she had not had the opportunities of her husband. However, she seems to have been led by these words into a true faith; for it is said, "By faith also Sarah herself received strength to conceive seed, and was delivered of a child when she was past age, because she judged Him faithful who had promised" (Heb. 11 : 11).

THIS IS THE TRUE LAW OF FAITH.—Do not look at your faith or at your feelings; but look away to the word of promise, and, above all, to the Promiser. Study the punctuality of His orderings in the starry firmament. Are planets ever overdue? or do the seasons forget to revolve? Consider how accurately He has kept His word with the nations of the past, whose ruined cities attest His judgments! Has He ever failed to keep His word? Is there any conceivable reason why He should not keep it? His power is omnipotent; and would He ever have pledged Himself to do what He could not effect? "He is faithful that promised."

Look from faith to the promise, and from the promise to the Promiser. And as we become conscious of possessing the power of vision whilst we look on any object to which we may direct our gaze, so we shall become conscious of the presence and the growth of faith as we look away to our faithful God.

"IS ANYTHING TOO HARD FOR THE LORD?"—That is one of God's unanswered questions. It has lain there for three thousand years, perused by myriads, answered by none; unless, indeed, those words of Jeremiah are the only answer which mortal men can give: "Ah, Lord God! behold, Thou hast made the heaven and the earth by Thy great power and stretched-out arm; and there is nothing too hard for Thee" (Jer. 32:17).

It may seem to you hard to the verge of impossibility, that ever God should keep his word, in the conversion of that friend for whom you have a warrant to pray, according to 1 John 5:16. Hard to vindicate your character from the aspersions with which it is being befouled. Hard to keep your evil nature in the place of death; and to cast down your evil imaginings, bringing every thought into captivity to the obedience of Christ. Hard to make you sweet and gentle, forgiving and loving. Hard to produce from you the fruits of a lovely and holy nature. It may be hard; but it is not too hard for the Lord. "With God all things are possible." And, as Sarah found it, all things are possible to those who believe.

The one thing that hinders God is our unbelief. Sarah must believe, and Abraham also, ere the child of promise could be born. And so must it be with us. As soon as we believe, then, according to our faith it is done to us; yea, exceeding abundantly beyond all we had asked or thought.

It may seem hard that the sins of a life should be forgiven; but God will do it for any penitent and believing soul. "All that believe in Christ are justified from all things" (Acts 13:39). It may seem hard that our naked souls should be attired in vestments fit for the royal palace; but it shall be so, if we have faith; for the righteousness of Christ is imputed and reckoned to all who believe (Rom. 3:22). It may seem hard that rebels should become children; yet this, too, shall be; for to them that receive Him He gives the right to become children of God (John 1:12).

You ask how to obtain this faith. Remember that faith is the receptive attitude of the soul, begotten and maintained by the grace of God. Christ is the Author and

Finisher of faith; not only in the abstract, but in the personal experience of the soul. Faith is the gift of God. If, then, you would receive it, put your will on the side of Christ; ñot a passing wish, but the whole will of your being: will to believe patiently, persistently, yearningly; let your eyes be ever toward the Lord; study the promises of God; consider the nature of God; be prepared to be rid of everything that grieves His Holy Spirit; and it is as certain as the truth of Christ, that you will have begotten and maintained in you the faith that can move mountains, and laugh at impossibilities.

And to such faith God will come, not as a passing wayfarer, but to abide; to feast with the soul in holy strengthening fellowship; to fill it with the true laughter; and to leave behind promises soon to become accomplished facts. "Behold, the tabernacle of God is with men, and He will dwell with them; and they shall be His people, and God Himself shall be with them, and be their God" (Rev. 21:3).

16

Pleading for Sodom

*And Abraham stood yet before the Lord; and
Abraham drew near."*—Genesis 18:22, 23.

As the day wore on, Abraham's mysterious guests went off
across the hills towards Sodom; and Abraham went with
them to bring them on their way. But all three did not
reach the guilty city, over which the thunder-clouds had
already commenced to gather. That evening two angels
entered it alone. And where was their companion? Ah! He
had stayed behind to talk yet further with His friend.
Tradition still points out the spot on the hills at the head
of a long steep ravine leading down to the sullen waters
of the Dead Sea where the Lord tarried behind to tell
Abraham all that was in his heart.

Why did not the Lord accompany His angels down to
Sodom? Was it because vengeance is His strange work,
in which He can take no pleasure? It surely befits the
dignity of the sovereign Judge to delegate to other hands
the execution of His decrees. "The Son of Man shall send
forth His angels, and they shall gather out of His Kingdom
all things that offend, and them that do iniquity" (Matt.
13:41).

But there was a deeper reason still. Abraham was the
"friend of God"; and friendship constitutes a claim to be
entrusted with secrets hidden from all beside. "The secret
of the Lord is with them that fear Him." "Henceforth,"
said the Master to His disciples, "I call you not servants;
for the servant knoweth not what his lord doeth; but I
have called you friends; for all things that I have heard
of My Father I have made known unto you" (John 15:15).
If we live near God, we shall have many things revealed to
us which are hidden from the wise and prudent. The
Septuagint version has well brought out the spirit of the
Divine reverie, when it puts the question thus: "Shall I
hide from Abraham, *my servant,* the thing which I do?"
The Lord does nothing which He does not first reveal to
His holy servants and prophets.

95

But the words which follow point to a yet further reason for the full disclosures that were made: "For I know him, that he will command his children and his household after him; and they shall keep the way of the Lord, to do justice and judgment" (Gen. 18:19). Was there a fear lest Abraham and his children might doubt the justice of the judgment of God if the righteous were summarily cut off with the wicked; and if the cities of the plain were destroyed without a revelation of their sin on the one hand, and the display of the Divine mercy on the other? Certainly it has placed the Divine character in an altogether different light, in that we have been permitted, in such a case as this, to understand some of the motives which have actuated God in His goodness or severity. And though His judgments must ever be a great deep, yet such a wondrous colloquy as this shines above them; as the rainbow trembles in its matchless beauty over the steamy depths of Niagara's plunge.

(1) THE BURDEN OF THE DIVINE ANNOUNCEMENT.—"The cry of Sodom and Gomorrah is great." What marvellous expression is this! There, far down the valley, bathed in the radiance of the westering sun, lay the guilty cities, still and peaceful. No sound travelled to the patriarch's ear, not even the roar which aeronauts detect in the dizzy heights of air, through which they travel on their adventurous way, passing mighty cities far beneath, which betray their existence by their voice. Quiet though Sodom seemed in the far distance, and in the hush of the closing day; yet to God there was a cry. The cry of the earth compelled to carry such a scar. The cry of inanimate creation, groaning and travailing in pain. The cry of the oppressed, the down-trodden—the victims of human violence and lust. The cry of the maiden, the wife, and the child. These were the cries which had entered into the ears of the Lord God of Sabaoth. And each sin has a cry. "The voice of thy brother's blood crieth unto Me." And it will go on crying; unless it is silenced by the yet greater voice of the blood of Christ, "which speaketh better things." And, if each sin has a cry, what must not be the volume of sound for a life, and for a city! Must not God still have to say of our great cities, one by one?—"Its cry is great; and its sin is very grievous."

"I will go down now, and see." God always narrowly investigates the true condition of the case, before He awards or executes His sentences. He comes seeking fruit for three years, before He gives the order for the cutting down of the tree that cumbered the vineyard soil. He

walks our streets day and night. He patrols our thorough-
fares, marking everything, missing nothing. He glides unasked into our most sacred privacy; for all things are
naked and open unto the eyes of Him with whom we have
to do. He is prepared, nay, eager to give us the benefit of
any excuse. But flagrant sin, like that which broke out in
Sodom that very night, is enough to settle for ever the
fate of a Godless community when standing at the bar of
Him who is Judge and Witness both.

"And if not, I will know." There was something very
ominous in all these words, which Abraham clearly understood to indicate the approaching destruction of the place;
for in his prayer he again and again alludes to the
imminence of its doom: "Wilt Thou, also, destroy the
righteous with the wicked?" But what is there that God
does not know? "The darkness and the light are both
alike to Him." Yet He says, "I will know." Yes, ungodly
man who mayest read this page: remember that from
God no secrets can be hid. He will search out the most
hidden ramifications of thy sin; bringing them out before
the gaze of the universe; and justifying His righteous
judgments which He will not spare.

(2) THE IMPRESSION WHICH THIS ANNOUNCEMENT MADE
ON ABRAHAM'S MIND.—So soon as the angels had gone on,
leaving Abraham alone with the Lord, he was thoroughly
aroused by the revelation which had broken upon him;
and his mind was filled with a tumult of emotion. He hardly
dared expostulate with God: what was he, but "dust and
ashes"? And yet he was impelled to make some attempt to
avert the doom that threatened the cities of the plain.

The motives that prompted him were twofold: (i) *There
was a natural anxiety about his kinsman, Lot.*—Twenty
years had passed since Lot had left him; but he had never
ceased to follow him with the most tender affection. He
could not forget that he was the son of his dead brother
Haran; or that he had been his ward; or that he had braved
the hardships of the desert in his company. All this had
been present to his mind, when, a few years before, he had
made a heroic effort to extricate him from the hands of
Chedorlaomer. And now the strong impulse of natural
affection stirred him to make one strenuous effort to save
Sodom; lest his nephew might be overwhelmed in its overthrow. Real religion tends not to destroy, but to fulfil all
the impulses of true natural love.

(ii) *There was also a fear lest the total destruction of*

*the cities of the plain might prejudice the character of God
in the minds of the neighbouring peoples.*—Abraham did
not deny that the fate which was about to overtake them
was deserved by many of the people of that enervating
and luxuriant valley: but he could not bring his mind to
suppose that the whole of the population was equally
debased; and he feared that if all were summarily swept
away, the surrounding nations would have a handle of
reproach against the justice of his God, and would accuse
Him of unrighteousness, inasmuch as He destroyed the
righteous with the wicked.

The character of God has ever been dear to his true-
hearted servants of every age. Moses was prepared to
forego the honour of being the ancestor of the chosen
people, rather than that the nations which had heard of
the Divine fame should be able to say that God was not
able to bring them into the Land of Promise.[1] And when
the men of Israel fled before Ai, Joshua and the elders
appear to have thought less of the danger of an immediate
rising to cut them off than of what God would do for His
great name. Oh for more of this chivalrous devotion to the
interests and glory of our God! Would that we were so
absorbed in all that touches the honour of the Divine
name amongst men, that this might be the supreme element
in our anxiety, as we view the drift of human opinion
concerning the enactments of Divine providence!

This passion for the glory of God burnt with a clear
strong flame in Abraham's heart; and it was out of this
that there arose his wondrous intercession. And when we
become as closely identified with the interests of God as
he was, we shall come to feel as he did; and shall be
eager that the Divine character should be vindicated
amongst the children of men; content, if need be, to lie
dying in the ditch, so long as we can hear the shouts of
triumph amid which our King rides over us to victory.

(3) THE ELEMENTS IN ABRAHAM'S INTERCESSION.—*It was
lonely prayer.*—He waited till on all that wide plateau,
and beneath those arching skies, there was no living man
to overhear this marvellous outpouring of a soul over-
charged, as are the pools, when, after the rains of spring,
they overflow their banks. "He stood before the Lord." It
is fatal to all the intensest, strongest devotion to pray
always in the presence of another, even the dearest. Every
saint must have a closet, of which he can shut the door,
and in which he can pray to the Father which is in secret.
The oratory may be the mountains, or the woods, or the

sounding shore; but it must be somewhere. Pitiable is the man who cannot—miserable the man who dare not—meet God face to face, and talk with Him of His ways, and plead for his fellows.

> *"For what are men better than sheep or goats,*
> *That nourish a blind life within the brain,*
> *If, knowing God, they lift not hands of prayer*
> *Both for themselves and those who call them friend."*

It was prolonged prayer.—"Abraham stood yet before the Lord." The story takes but a few moments to read; but the scene may have lasted for the space of hours. We cannot climb the more elevated pinnacles of prayer in a hasty rush. They demand patience, toil, prolonged endeavour, ere the lower slopes can be left, and the brooding cloud-line passed, and the aspiring soul can reach that cleft in the mountain side, where Moses stood beneath the shadow of God's hand. Of course, our God is ever on the alert to hear and answer those prayers which, like minute-guns, we fire through the live-long day; but we cannot maintain this posture of ejaculatory prayer unless we cultivate the prolonged occasions. How much we miss because we do not wait before God! We do not give the sun a chance to thaw us. We do not linger long enough upon the quay to see the vessels return freighted with the answers we had been praying for. If only we had remained longer at the palace door, we might have seen the King come out with a benediction in His face and a largess in His hands.

It was very humble prayer.—"Behold, now, I have taken upon me to speak unto the Lord, which am but dust and ashes." "Oh let not the Lord be angry, and I will speak." "Behold, I have taken upon me to speak unto the Lord." "Oh let not the Lord be angry, and I will speak yet but this once." The nearer we get to God, the more conscious are we of our own unworthiness; just as the higher a bird flies in mid-heaven, the deeper will be the reflection of its snowy pinions in the placid mere beneath. Let the glow-worm vie with the meridian sun; let the dewdrop boast itself against the fulness of the ocean bed; let the babe vaunt its knowledge with the intelligence of a seraph—before the man who lives in touch with God shall think of taking any other position than that of lowliest humiliation and prostration in His presence. Before Him angels veil their faces, and the heavens are not clean in His sight. And is it not remarkable that our sense of weakness is one of our strongest claims and arguments with God? "He forgetteth not the cry of the humble." "To that man will I look who trembleth."

This prayer was based on a belief that God possessed the same moral institutions as himself.—"Wilt Thou destroy the righteous with the wicked? That be far from Thee that the righteous should be as the wicked!" "Shall not the Judge of all the earth do right?" There is an infinite interest in this. It is as if the patriarch looked up from the clear depths of his own integrity into the azure heights of the Divine Being, and saw there enthroned a moral nature, at least as upright, fair, and true as his own; and to that he made his appeal, sure of a favourable response.

It was as if he had said: "Almighty God, I could not think it right to destroy the righteous with the wicked; and I am sure that any number of righteous men would shrink from doing so. And if this is binding on man, of course it must be much more binding on Thee, because Thou art the Judge of all the earth." And God was not angry; indeed He assented to Abraham's plea. And may we not go further, and say?—that though God may act in ways above our reason, yet He will not contradict those instincts of the moral sense which He has placed within our hearts. And if at times He seem to do so, it is because we have falsely conceived of His dealings, and put an erroneous interpretation upon them.

It was a cherished motto of bygone days that "the king could do no wrong." Alas! it was a vain dream. But what was untrue of the Stuarts is literally true of the Eternal God. He cannot outrage the moral nature in man, which is made in the likeness of His own. Let us possess our souls in patience, sure that any appearances to the contrary are the mists generated by our own evil natures or limited intelligence, and will be swept away from obscuring that everlasting righteousness which is steadfast and changeless as the great mountains.

This prayer was persevering.—Six times Abraham returned to the charge, and as each petition was granted, his faith and courage grew; and, finding he had struck a right vein, he worked it again, and yet again. It looks at first sight as if he forced God back from point to point, and wrung his petitions from an unwilling hand. But this is a mistake. In point of fact, *God was drawing him on*; and if he had dared to ask at first what he asked at the last, he would have got more than all that he asked or thought at the very commencement of his intercession. This was the time of his education. He did not learn the vast extent of God's righteousness and mercy all at once; he climbed the dizzy heights step by step; and, as he gained each step, he was inspired to dare another. What a pity that he stopped at ten! There is no knowing what he might have reached, had he gone on. As it was, the Almighty was obliged, by the demands of His own nature, to exceed the limits placed by Abraham, in bringing out of Sodom the only persons that could, by any possibility, be accounted "righteous."

It is so that God educates us still. In ever-widening circles, He tempts his new-fledged eaglets to try the sustaining elasticity of the air. He forces us to ask one thing; and then another, and yet another. And when we have asked our utmost, there are always unexplored remainders behind; and He does exceeding abundantly above all. There were not ten righteous men in Sodom; but Lot and his wife, and his two daughters, were saved, though three of them were deeply infected with the moral contagion of the place. And God's righteousness was clearly established and vindicated in the eyes of the surrounding peoples.

In closing, we remark *one of the great principles in the Divine government of the world.*—A whole city had been spared, if ten righteous men had been found within its walls. Ungodly men little realize how much they owe to the presence of the children of God in their midst. Long ere now had the floods of deserved wrath swept them all away; but judgment has been restrained, because God could not do anything while the righteous were found amongst them. The impatient servants have often asked if they should not gather out the tares. But the answer of the righteous Lord has ever been: "Nay, lest while ye gather up the tares, ye root up the wheat also with them." Ah, how little the world realizes the debt it owes to its saints, the salt to stay its corruption, the light to arrest the re-institution of the reign of chaos and night! We cannot but yearn over the world, as it rolls on its way towards its sad dark doom. Let us plead for it from the heights above Mamre. And may we and our beloved ones be led out from it into safety, ere the last plagues break full upon it in inevitable destruction!

NOTE

[1] See Exod. 32. 10; Num. 14. 12.

17

Angel Work in a Bad Town

(Genesis 19)

The waters of the Dead Sea ripple over a part of the site where once stood the cities of the plain, with their busy stir of life, and thought, and trade. But all the sounds of human joy, sorrow, or industry, the tread of the soldier, the call of the herdsman, the murmur of the market, the voices of little children playing in the open spaces—*all* are hushed in that awful solitude, the aspect of which is a striking testimony to the truth of the inspired Word.

Embosomed in gaunt mountains, the Dead Sea lies thirteen hundred feet below the level of the Mediterranean Sea. So weird and desolate is the scene, that it was long believed that no birds would fly across the sullen waters; no shells line the strand; no trace of living verdure is found along the shores: but, strewn along the desolate margin lie trunks and branches of trees, torn from the thickets of the river jungle by the violence of the Jordan, borne rapidly into the Sea of Sodom, and cast up again from its depths, encrusted with the salt which makes those waters utterly unfit to drink. And as the traveller wanders around the spot, he is irresistibly reminded of the time, when "the Lord rained upon Sodom and upon Gomorrah brimstone and fire from the Lord out of heaven; and He overthrew those cities, and all the plain, and all the inhabitants of the cities, and that which grew upon the ground."

THE REASONS WHICH JUSTIFIED THIS SUPREME ACT OF DESTRUCTION:

(1) *It was a merciful warning to the rest of mankind.*— The lesson of the Flood had well-nigh faded from the memory of man; and, heedless of all restraint, the human family had made terrible advances in the course of open shameless vice—so much so that there seemed an imminent danger of men repeating the abominable crimes that had opened the sluices of the Deluge. It was surely, therefore,

wise and merciful to set up a warning, which told its own terrible story, and reminded transgressors that there were limits beyond which the Judge of all the earth would not permit them to go.

It is true that the visitation, if it temporarily alarmed the nations of the immediate neighbourhood, did not prevent them from reaching a similar excess of immorality some centuries later, or from incurring at the edge of Joshua's sword the doom which heaven's fire had executed on their neighbours in the Jordan plain. Still, God's warnings have a merciful intention, even where they are unheeded; and this Sodom catastrophe has been well said to belong to that class of terrors in which a wise man will trace "the loving-kindness of the Lord."

(2) *Moreover, in this terrible act the Almighty simply hastened the result of their own actions.*—Nations are not destroyed until they are rotten at the core; as the north-east wind which snaps the forest trees only hastens the result for which the borer-worm had already prepared. It would have been clear to any thoughtful observer who had ventured out after dark in Sodom that it must inevitably fall. Unnatural crime had already eaten out the national heart, and, in the ordinary course of events, utter collapse could not be long delayed.

Go into the tents of Abraham, and you find simplicity; hospitality; the graces of a truly noble character, which guarantee the perpetuity of his name, and the glorious future of his children. Now go to Sodom: and in that sultry climate you find a population enervated with luxury; debased by cowardly submission to a foreign tyrant; cankered to the core with vice; not ten righteous men among them all; whilst the purity and sanctity of home are idle words. All these symptoms prognosticate, with prophetic voice, that their "sentence lingereth not, and their destruction slumbereth not."

This suggests a solemn lesson for ourselves. The tide of empire has ever set westwards. India, Babylon, Egypt, Greece, and Rome, have successively wielded supreme power, and sunk into oblivion. Shall it depart from Britain, as it has departed from the rest? It need not do so. Yet, as we remark the increase of extravagance and luxury; the reckless expenditure on pleasure; the shameless vice that flaunts itself in our streets; the adulation of wealth, the devotion to gambling which so largely supports the weekly and daily Press; the growing laxness of the marriage tie—we may well entertain the darkest fears about the future of our fatherland. The only hope for us is based on the important part which we are called to play in facilitating the evangelization of the world. Should we once fail in this—or should we send out more opium chests than Bibles, more spirit-sellers than missionaries—nothing can avert our fall.

(3) *Besides, this overthrow only happened after careful investigation.*—"I will go down now and see." Beneath these simple words we catch a glimpse of one of the most sacred principles of Divine action. God does not act hastily, nor upon hearsay evidence; He must see for Himself if there may not be some mitigating or extenuating circumstances. It was only after He had come to the fig-tree for many years, seeking fruit in vain, that He said, "Cut it down: why cumbereth it the ground?" And this deliberation is characteristic of God. He is unwilling that any should perish. He is slow to anger. Judgment is His strange work. He tells us that some day, when we come to look into his doings, we shall be comforted, concerning many of the evils which He has brought on the world, because we shall know that He has not done *without cause* all that He has done (Ezek. 14:23).

(4) *There is this consideration also—that, during the delay, many a warning was sent.*—First, there was the conquest by Chedorlaomer, some twenty years before the time of which we write. Then there was the presence of Lot, which, indeed, was enfeebled by his inconsistencies, but was yet a protest on the behalf of righteousness (2 Pet. 2:7, 8). Finally, there was the deliverance and restoration by the energetic interposition of Abraham. Again and again had God warned the men of these cities of their inevitable doom, if they did not repent. To use His own expressive words, He "rose up early" to send His messengers; but the people would not hear.

Nor is His usage different in the case of individuals. The course of every sin is against a succession of menacing red lights and exploding fog signals, warning of danger if that course be pursued. Just as the quivering of the nerves tells when the system is overstrained, and demands immediate rest at the risk of certain paralysis, if that warning be disregarded; so has God arranged that no downward step can be taken, without setting going vast numbers of shrill bells that tell of danger ahead. Transgressor! the signals are all against thee.

To regard these alarm tokens is to be saved. To disregard them, persevering in spite of all, is to deaden the soul and harden the heart, and run the risk of blasphemy against the Holy Ghost. For that unpardonable sin is not an act, but a state—the condition of the soul that does not, and cannot, feel; that it is utterly insensible and careless of its state; that drifts heedless to its doom; and is not forgiven, simply because it does not admit or feel its need of forgiveness, and, therefore, does not ask for it.

(5) *It is worthy of notice that God saved all whom He could.*—Lot was a sorry wreck of a noble beginning. When he started forth, as Abraham's companion from Ur, he gave promise of a life of quite unusual power and fruit. But he was one of those characters which cannot stand success. There is no temptation more insidious or perilous than that. The Enchanted Ground is more to be dreaded than the open assaults of Apollyon. More are ruined by the deceitfulness of riches than by the cares of life.

When first Lot went down to Sodom, attracted by the sole consideration of its pastures, it was no doubt his intention to keep aloof from its people, and to live without its walls. But the moth cannot with impunity flutter about the flame. By and by he abandoned the tent life altogether, and took a house inside the city. At last he betrothed his daughters to native Sodomites, and sat in its gateway as one of its aldermen. He was given to hospitality; but in the proposals by which he endeavoured to vindicate its exercise, he proved how the air of Sodom had taken the bloom off his purity. He was with difficulty dragged out of Sodom, as a brand plucked from the burning; and over the closing scenes of his life it is decent to draw a veil. And yet such a wreck was saved!

Nor was he saved alone; but his wife also, who did not take many steps outside the city, before, by looking back, with a mixture of disobedience and regret, she showed herself utterly hopeless; and her two daughters, whose names are branded with eternal infamy. If God was so careful to secure their safety, how bad must those have been whom He left to their fate! Is it not clear that He saved all who at all came within the range of mercy's possibilities? There will not be one soul amongst the lost who had the faintest claim to be among the saved; and there will be a great many among the saved whose presence there will be a very great surprise to us. "They shall come from the east and west...but the children of the kingdom shall be cast out."

THE MOTIVE OF THE ANGELS' VISIT.—These were three: (1) *The proximate, or nearest cause was their own love to man.*—The angels love us. Though they know that we are destined to a dignity before which that of the loftiest seraphs must pale, no envy eats out the pure benevolence which throbs within their holy spirits. It is enough that God has willed it so, and that we are dear to their sweet Master, Christ. It is then no hardship for them to leave "their golden bowers," or "cleave the flitting skies," that they may come and hasten lingerers to repentance. If there were any hardship, it would be in their mission to destroy.

(2) *The efficient cause was Abraham's prayer.*—"And it came to pass when God destroyed the cities of the plain, that God remembered Abraham, and sent Lot out of the midst of the overthrow" (Gen. 19:29). Pray on. beloved reader, pray on for that dear one far away in the midst of a very Sodom of iniquity. It may seem impossible for you to go down into it for his rescue, or to help him in any other way; but, in answer to your prayer, God will send His angels to that ship labouring in mid-ocean; into that log-house in the Canadian clearing, or that shanty by an African diamond mine; or away to that abode dedicated to vice or drink. God's angels go everywhere. A Sodom cannot hold its victims back from their touch, any more than their bright presences can be soiled by the polluting atmosphere through which they pass. Whilst you are praying, God's angels are on their way to perform your desire, albeit that their progress may be hindered by causes hidden from our ken (*see* Dan 10:12).

(3) *But the ultimate cause was God's mercy.*—"The Lord being merciful to him." Mercy: that is the last link in the chain. Is it not the staple in the wall? There is nothing beyond it. The Apostle himself cannot allege a more comprehensive or satisfactory reason for his position in the sunlit circle of salvation than this: "I obtained mercy." "By the grace of God, I am what I am." And this shall be our theme also through that eternity whose day-star has already arisen in our hearts.

It seems marvellous that God should employ sons of men to win men to Himself. Surely angels could do it better! Nay, did they not save Lot with a pertinacity, and a holy ingenuity, which are full of teaching and stimulus to ourselves, as workers for the Lord? The world is full of Sodoms still; and Lots, whom we have known and loved or who have a claim on us, are sitting at their gates. Oh, why are we behind the angels in eagerness to pluck them as brands from the burning? Bright spirits, ye shall read us some holy lessons as to methods of Christian work; and we shall try and emulate you—lest the time should come when we shall be dismissed from our posts;

and heaven's doors flung wide open each dawn to let out your rejoicing crowds, to take our place in class, or pulpit, or squalid court!

THE ANGELS WENT TO WHERE LOT WAS.—"There came two angels to Sodom at even." What! did angels go to Sodom? Yes, to Sodom—and yet angels. And as a ray of light may pass through the fœtid atmosphere of some squalid court, and emerge without a stain on its pure texture, so may angels spend a night in Sodom, surrounded by crowds of sinners, and yet be untainted angel still. If you go to Sodom for your gains, as Lot did, you will soon show signs of moral pollution. But if you go to save men, as these angels did, you may go into a very hell of evil, where the air is laden with impurity and blasphemy, but you will not be befouled. No grain of mud shall stick. "No weapon that is formed against thee shall prosper; and every tongue that shall rise against thee in judgment thou shalt condemn" (Isa. 54:17).

This is the spirit of Christ's Gospel. "He goeth after that which is lost till He find it." "He put forth His hand and touched him" (Luke 15:4; Matt. 8:3). We must not wait for sinners to come to us; we must go to them—to the banks of the stream, where the fish hide in the dark, cool depths; to the highways of the town, where men congregate; to public-houses, music-halls, stews of crime, and homes of poverty; yea, and to the most distant parts of the world—wherever men are found we must go to them, to preach the Gospel. The most unlikely places will yield Lots, who would have died in their sins, if they had not been sought out.

THEY WERE CONTENT TO WORK FOR VERY FEW.—Special value attaches to hand-picked fruit. Too often we, in our ignorance, prefer to go into the orchard and shake down from the trees the abundant crop, until the ground far and near is littered with fruit. But we forget how much waste there is in the process; and how much of the crop becomes bruised: whilst some is torn prematurely from the parent bough.

So far as we can gather, all our Lord's choicest followers were the result of His personal ministry. To one and another He said, "Follow Me!" His life was full of personal interviews. He sought out individual souls (Matt. 4:19, 21; 9:9; Luke 14:5). He would spend much time and thought to win one solitary woman, her character none too good (John 4). He believed in going after one sheep that was lost. And the steadfastness of their characters vindicated His methods. And it is most beautiful to trace the same characteristic in the Apostle Paul, who says that he "warned every man, and taught every man, that he might present every man perfect in Christ Jesus" (Col. 1:28).

It is a question whether more men are not saved by individual appeal than by all our preaching. It is not the sermon which wins them; but the quiet talk with a worker at an after-meeting, or the letter of a parent, or the words of a friend. When Christ said, "Preach the Gospel to every creature," did He not suggest that we were to set ourselves to the work of leaving the proclamation of heaven's love at every door, and to every child of Adam, throughout the world?

We never know what we do when we win one soul for God. Is not the following instance, culled from the biography of James Brainerd Taylor—called home to God too early, and yet not before he had won hundreds of souls by his personal appeals—a fair specimen of myriads more?

On one occasion he reined up his horse to drink at a roadside well. Another horseman at the same moment did the same. The servant of God, as the horses were eagerly quenching their thirst, turned to the stranger, and spoke some burning words concerning the duty and honour of Christian discipleship. In a moment more they had parted, and were riding in different directions. But the word of God remained as incorruptible seed, and led to the conversion of that wayside hearer. He became a Christian and a missionary. Often he wondered who had been the instrument of his conversion, and sought for him in vain. But he did not succeed in identifying him till years after, when, in a packet of books, sent him from his native land, he opened the story of that devoted life, and in the frontispiece beheld the face which had haunted him, in sleeping and waking hours, ever since that slight but memorable interview.

It has been said that the true method of soul-winning is to set the heart on some one soul; and to pursue it, until it has either definitely accepted, or finally rejected, the Gospel of the grace of God. We should not hear so many cries for larger spheres, if Christians only realized the possibilities of the humblest life. Christ found work enough in a village to keep Him there for thirty years. Philip was torn from the great revival in Samaria to go into the desert to win one seeker after God.

Have you ever spoken to your servant, your shoeblack,

your postman, your companion, your neighbour? Ah, it would not take long to evangelize the world, if every man would teach his neighbour, and every man his brother, saying, "Know the Lord!"

THEY TOLD LOT PLAINLY OF HIS DANGER.—"Hast thou here any besides? ... bring them out of this place: for we will destroy this place, because the cry of them is waxen great before the face of the Lord; and the Lord hath sent us to destroy it" (Gen. 19:12, 13). We are rather squeamish nowadays of talking to men thus. We have lined our lips with velvet. We aim to be gentler than Christ. He did not hesitate to speak of an undying worm and a quenchless flame. The gnashing of teeth; the wail of despair; the knock to which no door would open—were arguments which came more than once from His lips. (See Matt. 8:12; 13:42, 50; 22:13; 24:51; 25:10-12, 30; Mark 9:43-48; Luke 13:25-28). He evidently taught as if men might make a mistake which they could not possibly repair. If certain elements are wanting in food, the children will grow up boneless and unhealthy; and if we do not take care, the deficiency of our modern teaching will have disastrous results. Whether we talk about it or not, it is yet as true as the nature of God, that those who obey not the Gospel of our Lord Jesus Christ "shall be punished with everlasting destruction from the presence of the Lord, and from the glory of His power" (2 Thess. 1:9). And "if we sin wilfully after that we have received the knowledge of the truth, there remaineth no more sacrifice for sins, but a certain fearful looking-for of judgment and fiery indignation, which shall devour the adversaries" (Heb. 10:26, 27).

It may be that the day of grace is nearer to its close than we think. The clock of destiny may have struck; the avalanche may have commenced to roll forward its overwhelming mass; whilst the storm-clouds may brood heavily over a godless age, for which, in the Day of Judgment, it shall be worse than for Sodom and Gomorrah. There may be nothing to portend this momentous fact. "The sun was risen upon the earth when Lot entered into Zoar." Nature keeps God's secrets well. No portent in heaven, no driving up of the cloud-wrack in the clouds, no tremor on earth; but the axe suddenly driven home to the heart of the doomed tree. Escape, my reader, for thy life; look not behind thee, neither stay thou anywhere short of the cleft side of Jesus, where only we may hide from the just judgment of sin. Rest not till thou hast put the Lord Jesus between thyself and the footsteps of pursuing justice.

THEY HASTENED HIM.—"When the morning arose, then the angels hastened Lot" (19:15). They had been reluctant to stay in his house, unlike the alacrity with which they accepted Abraham's hospitality; and they spent the short sultry night in urging on Lot the certainty and terror of the approaching destruction. So much so that they actually got him to go to arouse his sons-in-law. But an inconsistent life cannot arrest the wanderer, or startle the sleeper into wide-awakeness about his soul. People say that we must conform a little to the manners of our time, if we would exert a saving influence over men. It is a fatal mistake. If we live in Sodom, we shall have no power to save the people of Sodom. You must stand outside of them, if you would save them from the gurgling rapids. Yes, dwellers in Sodom, you cannot level Sodom up; but it will certainly level you down, and laugh at you, when you try to speak. "He seemed as one that mocked unto his sons-in-law."

But when he came back from his ineffectual mission, Lot seemed infected by the scepticism which had ridiculed his warnings. "He lingered." How could he leave his children, and household goods, and property, on what seemed to be a fool's errand? Surely all things would continue as they had been from the beginning of the world. "And while he lingered, the men laid hold upon his hand."

It was hand-help. It was the urgency of love that would take no denial. The two angels had four hands, but each hand was full, and each clasped the hand of a procrastinating sinner. Would that we knew more fully this divine enthusiasm, which pulls men out of the fire! (Jude 23).

Nor were they satisfied, till their *protégés* were safe without the city; and were speeding towards the rampart of the distant hills. So Lot was saved from the overthrow. But though he was sent out of Sodom, he took Sodom with him; and over the remainder of his history we must draw a veil. Still, it is a marvellous testimony to the power of intercessory prayer, to learn that a man so low in the moral scale, together with his daughters, was saved for Abraham's sake; and if he had finally settled at the little city of Zoar, that too would have been spared for his sake.

Let us hasten sinners. Let us say to each one: "Escape for thy life; better lose all than lose your soul. Look not behind to past attainments or failures. Linger nowhere outside the City of Refuge, which is Jesus Christ Himself. Haste ye! habits of indecision strengthen; opportunities are closing in; the arrow of destruction has already left the bow of justice: "behold, now is the accepted time: behold, now is the day of salvation."

18

A Bit of the Old Nature

*Then Abimelech called Abraham, and said
unto him, What hast thou done unto us? and
what have I offended thee, that thou has
brought on me and on my kingdom a great
sin?*—Genesis 20:9.

For long years an evil may lurk in our hearts, permitted
and unjudged, breeding failure and sorrow in our lives,
as some unnoticed and forgotten sewer may secretly under-
mine the health of an entire household. In the twilight
we overlook many a thing which we should not allow for
a single moment if we saw it in its true character; and
which, amid the all-revealing light of the perfect day, we
should be the first to fling away in horror. But that which
escapes our ken is patent in all its naked deformity to
the eye of God. "The darkness and the light are both alike
to Him." And He will so direct the discipline of our
lives as to set in clear prominence the deadly evil which
He hates; so that, when He has laid bare the cancerous
growth, He may bring us to long for and invite the knife
which shall set us free from it for ever.

These words have been suggested by the thirteenth verse
of this chapter, which indicates an evil compact, into which
Abraham had entered with Sarah some thirty years before
the time of which we write. Addressing the king of the
Philistines, the patriarch let fall a hint which sheds a
startling light upon his failure, when first he entered the
Land of Promise, and, under stress of famine, went down
into Egypt; and upon that repetition of his failure which
we must now consider. Here is what he said: "And it
came to pass, when God caused me to wander from my
father's house, that I said unto my wife, This is thy kindness which thou shalt show unto me; at every place
whither we shall come, say of me, He is my brother."

In a certain sense, no doubt, Sarah was his sister. She
was the daughter of his father, though not the daughter
of his mother. But she was much more his wife than his

sister; and to withhold that fact was to withhold the one fact that was essential to the maintenance of his honour, and the protection of her virtue. We are not bound to tell the whole truth to gratify an idle curiosity; but we are bound not to withhold the one item, which another should know before completing a bargain, if the knowledge of it would materially alter the result. A lie consists in the motive quite as much as in the actual words. We may unwittingly say that which is actually false, meaning above all things to speak the truth, and, though a lie in form, there is no lie in fact. On the other hand, like Abraham, we may utter true words, meaning them to convey a false impression, and in the sight of Heaven we are guilty of a deliberate and shameful falsehood.

This secret compact between Abraham and his wife, in the earliest days of his exodus, was due to his slender faith in God's power to take care of them, which again sprang from his limited experience of his Almighty Friend. In this we may find its sole excuse. But it ought long before this to have been cancelled by mutual consent. The faithless treaty should have been torn into shreds, and scattered to the winds of heaven. It was not enough that they did not act on it for many years; for it was evidently still in existence, tacitly admitted by each of them, and only waiting for an emergency to arise from the dusty obscurity into which it had receded, and to come again into light and use.

But the existence of this hidden understanding, though perhaps Abraham did not realize it, was inconsistent with the relation into which he had now entered with God. It was altogether a source of weakness and failure. And, above all, it was a secret flaw in his faith, which would inevitably affect its tone, and destroy its effectiveness in the dark trials which were approaching. God could afford to pass it over in those early days, when faith itself was yet in germ; but it could not be permitted, when that faith was reaching to a maturity in which any flaw would be instantly detected; and it would be an unsuitable example in one who was to become the model of faith to the world.

The judgment and eradication of this lurking evil were therefore necessary, and were brought about in this wise.

The day before Sodom's fall, the Almighty told Abraham that, at a set time in the following year, he should have a son and heir. And we should have expected that he would have spent the slow-moving months beneath the oak of Mamre, already hallowed by so many associations. But such was not the case. It has been suggested that he was too horrified at the overthrow of the cities of the plain, to be able to remain any longer in the vicinity. All further association with the spot was distasteful to him. Or it may have been that another famine was threatening. But in any case "he journeyed from hence towards the south country, and dwelled between Kadesh and Shur, and sojourned in Gerar" (Gen. 20:1).

Gerar was the capital of a race of men who had dispossessed the original inhabitants of the land, and were gradually passing from the condition of wandering shepherd life into that of a settled and warlike nation; afterwards to be known to the Hebrews by the dreaded name, Philistines: a title which, in fact, gave to the whole land its name of Palestine. Their chieftain bore the official title of Abimelech, "My Father the King."

Here, the almost forgotten agreement between Sarah and himself offered itself as a ready expedient, behind which Abraham's unbelief took shelter. He knew the ungoverned license of his time, unbridled by the fear of God (ver. 11). He dreaded, lest the heathen monarch, enamoured with Sarah's beauty, or ambitious to get her into his power for purposes of State policy, might slay him for his wife's sake. And so he again resorted to the paltry policy of calling her his sister. As if God could not have defended him and her, screening them from all evil; as He had done so often in days gone by.

HIS CONDUCT WAS VERY COWARDLY.—He risked Sarah's virtue, and the purity of the promised seed. And, even if we accept the justification of his conduct proposed by some, who argue that he was so sure of the seed promised him by God that he could dare to risk what otherwise he would have more carefully guarded, his faith leading him into the license of presumption, yet, it was surely very mean on his part to permit Sarah to pass through any ordeal of the sort. If he had such superabundant faith, he might have risked his own safety at the hand of Abimelech rather than Sarah's virtue.

IT WAS ALSO VERY DISHONOURING TO GOD.—Amongst those untutored tribes Abraham was well known as the servant of Jehovah. And they could not but judge of the character of Him whom they could not see, by the traits they discerned in His servant, whom they knew in familiar intercourse. Alas that Abraham's standard was lower than their own! so much so that Abimelech was able to rebuke him, saying: "Thou hast brought on me and on my kingdom a great sin: thou hast done deeds unto me that ought not to be done." Such an opinion, elicited in such a way, must have been an unpropitious preparation for any attempt to proselytize Abimelech to the Hebrew faith. "Not so," we can image him saying: "I have had some experience of one of its foremost representatives, and I prefer to remain as I am."

It is heart-breaking, when the heathen rebukes a professor of superior godliness for speaking lies. Yet it is lamentable to confess that such men often enough have higher standards of morality than those who profess godliness. Even if they do not fulfil their own conceptions, yet the beauty of their ideal is undeniable, and is a remarkable vindication of the universal vitality of conscience. The temperate Hindu is scandalized by the drunkenness of the Englishman whose religion he is invited to embrace. The Chinaman cannot understand why he should exchange the hoary religion of Confucius for that of a people which by superior armaments forces upon his country a drug which is sapping its vitals. The employé abhors a creed which is professed by his master for one day of the week, but is disowned on the other six. Let us walk circumspectly towards them that are without; adorning in all things the Gospel of Jesus Christ; and giving no occasion to the enemy to blaspheme, save as it concerns the law of our God.

IT ALSO STOOD OUT IN POOR RELIEF AGAINST THE BEHAVIOUR OF ABIMELECH.—As to his original character, Abimelech commends himself to us as the nobler of the two. He rises early in the morning, prompt to set the great wrong right. He warns his people. He restores Sarah with munificent presents. His reproach and rebuke are spoken in the gentlest, kindest tones. He simply tells Sarah that her position as the wife of a prophet would, not in Philistia only, but wherever they might come, be a sufficient security and veil (ver. 16). There is the air of high-minded nobility in his behaviour throughout this crisis which is exceedingly winsome.

It would almost appear as if the Spirit of God took delight in showing that the original texture of God's saints was not higher than that of other men, nor indeed so high. What they became, they became in spite of their natural selves. So marvellous is the wonder-working power of the grace of God that He can graft His rarest fruits on the wildest stocks. He seems to delight to secure His choicest results in natures which men of the world might reject as hopelessly bad. He demands no assistance from us, so sure is He that when once faith is admitted as the root-principle of character, all other things will be added to it.

Oh, critics of God's handiwork, we do not deny the inconsistencies of a David, a Peter, or an Abraham; but we insist that those inconsistencies were not the result of God's work, but in spite of it. They indicate the hopelessness of the original nature—the moorland waste to which He has set His cultivating hand. And shall we blame the Gardener's skill, when, in the paradise which it has created, we encounter a bit of original soil, which, by force of contrast, indicates the marvel of His genius; and which, before long, if only we exercise patience, will yield to the self-same spell, and blossom as the rest?

And you, on the other hand, who aspire for the crown of saintliness, to which ye are truly called, take heart! There is nothing which God has done for any soul that He will not do for you. And there is no soil so unpromising that He will not compel it to yield His fairest results. "What is impossible to man is possible to God." The same power in all its matchless energy, which raised the body of our Lord from its sleep in the grave of Joseph, to sit at the Father's side in the heights of glory, in spite of opposing battalions of evil spirits—is ready to do as much for each of us, if only we will daily, hourly, yield to it without reserve. Only cease from your own works, and keep always on God's "lift," refusing each solicitation to step off its ascending energy, or to do for yourself what He will do for you so much better than you can ask or think.

Let us ponder, as we close, these practical lessons:

(1) WE ARE NEVER SAFE SO LONG AS WE ARE IN THIS WORLD.—Abraham was an old man. Thirty years had passed since that sin had shown itself last. During that time he had been growing and learning much. But, alas! the snake was scotched, not killed. The weeds were cut down, not eradicated. The dry-rot had been checked; but the rotten timbers had not been cut away. Never boast yourself against once-cherished sins: only by God's grace are they kept in check; and if you cease to abide in Christ, they will revive and revisit you, as the seven sleepers of Ephesus re-appeared to the panic-stricken town.

(2) WE HAVE NO RIGHT TO THROW OURSELVES INTO THE WAY OF THE TEMPTATION WHICH HAS OFTEN MASTERED US. —Those who daily cry, "Lead us not into temptation,"

should see to it that they do not court the temptation against which they pray. We must not expect angels to catch us every time we choose to cast ourselves from the mountain brow. A godly fear will avoid the perilous pass marked by crosses to indicate the failures of the past, and will choose a safer route. Abraham had been wiser had he never gone into the Philistines' territory at all.

(3) WE MAY BE ENCOURAGED BY GOD'S TREATMENT OF ABRAHAM'S SIN.—Although God had a secret controversy with His child, He did not put him away. And when his wife and he were in extreme danger, as the result of his sin, their Almighty Friend stepped in to deliver them from the peril which menaced them. Again "He reproved kings for their sakes, saying, Touch not My annointed, and do My prophets no harm." He told Abimelech that he was a dead man; put an arrest upon him by the ministry of an ominous disease; and bade him apply to the intercession of the very man by whom he had been so grievously misled, and who, in spite of all his failures, was a prophet still, having power with God.

Have you sinned, bringing disrepute on the name of God? Do not despair. Go alone, as Abraham must have done, and confess your sin with tears and childlike trust. Do not abandon prayer. Your prayers are still sweet to Him; and He waits to answer them. It is only through them that His purposes can be fulfilled toward men. Trust then in the patience and forgiveness of God, and let His love, as consuming fire, rid you of concealed and hidden sin.

19

Hagar and Ishmael Cast Out

*Cast out this bondwoman and her son: for
the son of this bondwoman shall not be heir
... with Isaac.*—Genesis 21 : 10.

Even though we were hearing this story for the first time,
and did not know of the grave crisis to which we were
approaching in the next chapter, we might be sure that
something of the sort was imminent; and we should rest
our conclusion on the fact of the stern discipline through
which the great patriarch was called to pass. Faith is
the expression of our inner moral life; and it cannot be
exercised in its loftiest form so long as there is any
obliquity of the heart, any hidden or unholy affection.
These things must be cut away, or passed through the
fiery discipline of sorrow; that, being freed from them,
the heart many exercise that supreme faith in God which
is the fairest crown of human existence.

The Almighty Lover of souls knew the trial which
awaited His child in the near future; and set Himself to
prepare him for it, by ridding him of certain clinging
inconsistencies, which would have paralysed the action of
his faith in the hour of trial. We have already seen how
one of these—the secret compact between himself and
Sarah—was exposed to the light and judged. We have now
to see how another matter, the patriarch's connection with
Hagar and her child, was also dealt with by Him, who acts
on us either as fuller's soap, or if that be not strong
enough, as a refiner's fire.

In what way the presence of Hagar and Ishmael hindered
the development of Abraham's noblest life of faith, we
cannot entirely understand. Did his heart still cling to the
girl who had given him his firstborn son? Was there any
secret satisfaction in the arrangement, which had at least
achieved one cherished purpose, though it had been un-
blessed by God? Was there any fear that if he were
summoned to surrender Isaac, he would find it easier to
do so, because, at any moment, he could fall back on

Ishmael, as both son and heir? We cannot read all that was in Abraham's mind; but surely some such thoughts are suggested by the expressions which to this hour record the history of the anguish of this torn and lonely heart, as one darling idol after another was rent away, that he himself might be cast naked and helpless on the omnipotence of the Eternal God. "The thing was very grievous in Abraham's sight" (*ver.* 11).

It may be that not a few who read these lines sigh to possess a faith like that which Abraham had: a faith which staggers not through unbelief; a faith to which God cannot give a denial; a faith which can open and shut heaven, and to which all things are possible. But are you willing to pay the cost?—the cost of suffering; the cost of rending from your heart all that would frustrate the operation of so glorious a principle; the cost of seeing one cherished idol after another cast out; the cost of being stripped even to nakedness of all the dear delights in which the flesh may have found pleasure. "Are ye able to drink of the cup that I shall drink of, and to be baptized with the baptism that I am baptized with? They say unto Him, We are able" (Matt. 20, 22; Mark 10:38, 39). You hardly realize all that is meant when you say so much; but it shall be revealed to you step by step; and nothing shall be too difficult, all being measured out according to your strength by Him who knows our frame and remembers that we are dust. Let us not dread the pruning-knife; for it is wielded by the hand of One who loves us infinitely, and who is seeking results that are to fill our hearts with eternal gratitude, and heaven with praise.

The final separation from Abraham of ingredients which would have been prejudicial to the exercise of a supreme faith was brought about by the birth of the long-promised child, which is alluded to at the commencement of this chapter (Gen. 21), and which led up to the crisis with which we are now dealing.

"The Lord visited Sarah as He had said, and the Lord did unto Sarah as He had spoken" (Gen. 21:1). It is impossible to trust God too absolutely. God's least word is a spar of imperishable wood driven into the Rock of Ages, which will never give, and on which you may hang your entire weight for evermore. "The counsel of the Lord standeth for ever; the thoughts of His heart to all generations (Psalm 33:11).

BUT WE MUST BE PREPARED TO WAIT GOD'S TIME.—"Sarah bare Abraham a son in his old age, *at the set time* of which God had spoken unto him." God has His set times. It is not for us to know them; indeed, we cannot know them; we must wait for them. If God had told Abraham in Haran that he must wait for thirty years until he pressed the promised child to his bosom, his heart would have failed him. So, in gracious love, the length of the weary years was hidden, and only as they were nearly spent, and there were only a few more months to wait, God told him that "according to the time of life, Sarah shall have a son" (18:14). The set time came at last; and then the laughter that filled the patriarch's home made the aged pair forget the long and weary vigil. "And Abraham called the name of his son that was born unto him, whom Sarah bare unto him, ISAAC" (*that is* LAUGHTER). Take heart, waiting one, thou waitest for One who cannot disappoint thee; and who will not be five minutes behind the appointed moment: ere long "your sorrow shall be turned into joy."

"A woman, when she is in travail, hath sorrow, because her hour is come: but as soon as she is delivered of the child, she remembereth no more the anguish, for joy that a man is born into the world" (John 16:21). That joy may give the clue to the unwonted outburst of song on the part of the happy and aged mother. The laughter of incredulity, with which she received the first intimation of her approaching motherhood (18:12), was now exchanged for the laughter of fulfilled hope. And she gave utterance to words that approached the elevation of a rhythmic chant, and which served as the model of that other song with which the virgin mother announced the advent of her Lord. So Sarah said,

> *"God hath made me to laugh:*
> *Every one that heareth will laugh with me."*

And long after, one of her daughters said,

> *"My soul doth magnify the Lord;*
> *And my spirit hath rejoiced*
> *In God my Saviour.*
> *For He that is mighty*
> *Hath done to me great things;*
> *And holy is His name."*
> LUKE 1:46–49.

Ah, happy soul, when God makes thee laugh! Then sorrow and crying shall flee away for ever, as darkness before the dawn.

The peace of Abraham's house remained at first unbroken, though there may have been some slight symptoms of the rupture which was at hand. The dislike which Sarah had manifested to Hagar, long years before, had never been extinguished: it had only smouldered in her bosom, waiting for some slight incident to stir it again into a blaze. Nor had the warm passionate nature of Hagar ever forgotten those hard dealings which had driven her forth, to fare as best she might in the inhospitable desert. Abraham must have been often sorely put to it to keep the peace between them. At last the women's quarters could conceal the quarrel no longer, and the scandal broke out into the open day.

THE IMMEDIATE OCCASION OF THIS OPEN RUPTURE was the weaning of the young Isaac. "The child grew, and was weaned: and Abraham made a great feast the day that Isaac was weaned." But amid all the bright joy of that happy occasion, one shadow suddenly stole over the scene, and brooded on the mother's soul. Sarah's jealous eye saw Ishmael mocking. It was hardly to be wondered at. The lad had recently suffered a severe disappointment. He had grown up as the undisputed heir of all that camp, accustomed to receive its undivided loyalty; and it must have been very difficult to view with equanimity the preparations made in honour of the child who was destined to supersede him: and so, under the appearance of sportive jesting, he jeered at Isaac in a way which betrayed the bitterness of his soul; and which indeed he was at no pains to conceal. This awoke all Sarah's slumbering jealousy; which may often have been severely tested during the last few years by Ishmael's assumption and independent bearing. She would stand it no longer. Why should she, the chieftain's wife, and mother of his heir, brook the insolence of a slave? And so she said unto Abraham with a sneer and the sting of the old jealousy, "Cast out this bondwoman and her son; for the son of this bondwoman shall not be heir with my son, even with Isaac."

WE CANNOT BUT RECALL THE USE WHICH THE GREAT APOSTLE MAKES OF THIS INCIDENT.—In his days the Jews, priding themselves on being the lineal descendants of Abraham, refused to consider it possible that any but themselves could be children of God, and the heirs of promise. They arrogated to themselves exclusive privileges and position. And when large numbers of Gentiles were born into the Christian Church under the first preaching of the Gospel, and claimed to be the spiritual seed, with all the rights pertaining thereunto; they who, like Ishmael, were simply born after the flesh, persecuted them which, like Isaac, were born after the Spirit. Everywhere the Jews set themselves to resist the preaching of the Gospel, which denied to them their exclusive privileges; and to harry those who would not enter the Church through the rites of Judaism. And ere long the Jewish nation was rejected; put aside; cast out. Succeeding ages have seen the building-up of the Church from among the once-persecuted ones, whilst the children of Abraham have wandered in the wilderness fainting for the true water of life (Gal. 4:29).

BUT THERE IS A STILL DEEPER REFERENCE.—Hagar, the slave, who may even have been born in the Sinaitic Desert, with which she seems to have been so familiar, is a fit representative of the spirit of legalism and bondage, seeking to win life by the observance of the law, which was given from those hoary cliffs. Hagar is the covenant of Mount Sinai in Arabia, "which gendereth to bondage," and "is in bondage with her children" (Gal. 4:24, 25). Sarah, the free woman, on the other hand, represents the covenant of free grace. Her children are love, and faith, and hope; they are not bound by the spirit of "must," but by the promptings of spontaneous gratitude; their home is not in the frowning clefts of Sinai, but in Jerusalem above, which is free, and is the mother of us all. Now, argues the Apostle, there was no room for Hagar and Sarah, with their respective children, in Abraham's tent. If Ishmael was there, it was because Isaac was not born. But as soon as Isaac came in, Ishmael must go out. So the two principles—of legalism, which insists on the performance of the outward rite of circumcision; and of faith, which accepts the finished work of the Saviour—cannot co-exist in one heart. It is a moral impossibility. As well could darkness co-exist with light, and slavery with freedom. So, addressing the Galation converts, who were being tempted by Judaising teachers to mingle legalism and faith, the Apostle bade them follow the example of Abraham, and cast out the spirit of bondage which keeps the soul in one perpetual agony of unrest.

You, my readers, are trusting Christ; but, perhaps, you are living in perpetual bondage to your scruples; or, perhaps you are always endeavouring to add some acts of obedience, by way of completing and assuring your salvation. Ah! it is a great mistake. Cease to worry about these legal matters. Beware of morbid scrupulosity of conscience, one of the most terrible diseases by which the human spirit can be plagued. Do not always imagine that God's love to you depends on the performance of many minute acts, concerning which there are no definite instructions given. Trust Christ. Realize His wonderful and complete salvation. Work not towards sonship, but from it. "Cast out the bondwoman and her son." Live the free, happy life of Isaac, whose position is assured; and not that of Ishmael, whose position is dependent on his good behaviour. "Thy servant abideth not in the house for ever; but the son abideth ever."

THE REMAINING HISTORY IS BRIEFLY TOLD.—With many a pang—the vine which bleeds copiously when the pruning knife is doing its work—Abraham sent Hagar and her child forth from his home, bidding them a last sad farewell. In the dim twilight they fared forth, before the camp was astir. The strong man must have suffered keenly as he put the bread into her hand, and with his own fingers bound the bottle of water on her shoulder, and kissed Ishmael once more. And yet he must not let Sarah guess how much he felt it. How many passages in our lives are only known to God!

Yet it was better so. And God provided for them both. When the mother's hopes were on the point of expiring, and the lad lay dying of thirst in the scorching noon, under the slender shade of a desert shrub, the Angel of God stayed her sobs, pointed out the well of water to which her tears had made her blind, and promised that her child should become a great nation. Ishmael would never have developed to his full stature if he had perpetually lived in the enervating luxury of Abraham's camp. There was not room enough there for him to grow. For him, as for us all, there was need of the free air of the desert, in which he should match himself with his peers, becoming strong by privation and want. That which seems like to break our hearts at the moment, turns out in after-years to have been of God. "And God said unto Abraham, Let it not be grievous in thy sight; in all that Sarah hath said unto thee, hearken unto her voice" (21 : 12).

One more weight was laid aside, and one more step taken in the preparation of God's "friend" for the supreme victory of his faith; for which his whole life had been a preparation, and which was now at hand.

Some flowers are the result of a century of growth; and the Divine Husbandman will consider Himself repaid for years of loving, patient care, if the life He has tended will bloom out into but one act, like that which we are soon to record. Such acts scatter the seeds of noble and heroic deeds for all future time.

20

A Quiet Resting Place

*And Abraham planted a grove in Beersheba,
and called there on the name of the Lord,
the everlasting God: and Abraham sojourned
in the Philistines' land many days.*—Genesis
21 : 33, 34.

When a river is approaching its plunge down some mighty
chasm, its waters flow with placid stillness; every ripple is
smoothed out of the peaceful surface, and the great volume
of water is hushed and quieted. There could hardly be a
greater contrast than that which exists between the restful-
ness of the river before it is torn by the ragged rocks in
its downward rush, and its excitement and foam at the
foot of the falls. In the one case you can discern, through
the translucent waters, the stones and rocks that line its
bed; in the other you are blinded by the spray and deafened
by the noise.

Is not this an emblem of our lives?—Our Father often
inserts in them a parenthesis of rest and peace, to prepare
us for some coming trial. It is not invariably so. We need
not always temper our enjoyment of some precious gift with
a foreboding dread of its *afterwards*. But this, at least, is
largely true: that if every season of clear-shining is not
followed by a time of cloud, yet seasons of sorrow and
trial are almost always preceded by hours or days or years
of sunny experience, which lie in the retrospect of life, as a
bright and comforting memory, where the soul was able
to gather the strength it was to expend, and to prepare
itself for its supreme effort.

Thus it happened to Abraham.—We have already seen
how wisely and tenderly his Almighty Friend had been
preparing him for his approaching trial; first, in searching
out his hidden compact with Sarah; and then in ridding
him of the presence of Hagar and her son. And now some
further preparation was to be wrought in his spirit, through
this period of peaceful rest beside the well of the oath.

Leaving Gerar, the patriarch travelled with his slow-moving flocks along the fertile valley, which extends from the sea into the country. The whole district was admirably suited for the maintenance of a vast pastoral clan. In the winter the valley contains a running stream, and at any time water may be obtained by digging at a greater or less depth. Having reached a suitable camping-ground, Abraham digged a well, which is probably one of those which remain to this day; and of which the water lying some forty feet below the surface, is pure and sweet. Drinking troughs for the use of cattle are scattered around in close proximity to the mouth, the kerbstones of which are deeply worn by the friction of the ropes used in drawing up the water by hand. It is not improbable that these very stones were originally hewn under the patriarch's direction, even though their position may have been somewhat altered by the Arab workmen of a later date.

Shortly after Abraham had settled there, Abimelech, the king, accompanied by Phichol, the chief captain of his host, came to his encampment, intent on entering into a treaty which should be binding, not only on themselves, but on their children: "Swear unto me here by God, that thou wilt not deal falsely with me, nor with my son, nor with my son's son" (*ver.* 23). Before formally binding himself under these solemn sanctions, Abraham brought up a matter which is still a fruitful subject of dispute in Eastern lands. The herdsman of Abimelech had violently taken away the well of water which the servants of Abraham had dug. But the king immediately repudiated all knowledge of their action. It had been done without his cognizance and sanction. And in the treaty into which the two chieftains entered, there was, so to speak, a special clause inserted with reference to this well, destined in after years to be so famous. Writing materials were not then in use; but the seven ewe lambs, which Abraham gave Abimelech, were the visible and lasting memorial that the well was his recognized property. Thus it happened that as the solemnly-sworn covenant was made beside the well, so its name became for ever associated with it, and it was called "Beer-sheba", the well of the oath, or "the well of the seven", with reference to the seven gifts, or victims, on which the oath was taken.

In further commemoration of this treaty, Abraham planted a tamarisk tree, which, as a hardy evergreen, would long perpetuate the memory of the transaction in those lands, where the mind of man eagerly catches at anything that will break the monotony of the landscape. There also he erected an altar, or shrine, and called on the name of the Lord, the Everlasting God. "And Abraham sojourned in the land of the Philistines many days." Ah! those long, happy days! Their course was only marked by the growing years of Isaac, who passed on through the natural stages of human growth—from boyhood to youth, and from youth to opening manhood—the object of Abraham's tender, clinging love. No words can tell the joy of Abraham over his beloved child of his old age. "Thine only son Isaac, whom thou lovest." It seemed as if perpetual laughter had come to take up its abode in that home, to brighten the declining years of that aged pair. Who could have foretold that the greatest trial of all his life had yet to come, and that from a clear sky a thunderbolt was about to fall, threatening to destroy all his happiness at a single stroke?

We none of us know what awaits us.—This at least is clear, that our life is being portioned out by the tender love of God; who spared not His own Son, and has pledged Himself, with Him, also freely to give up all things. Here is one of the unanswerable questions of Scripture: What will not God do for them that love Him? No love, no care, no wisdom, which they need, shall be spared. And yet, with all this, there may be keen suffering to bear. We sometimes seem to forget that what God takes He takes in fire: that nothing less than the discipline of pain can ever disintegrate the clinging dross of our natures; and that the only way to the resurrection life and the ascension mount is the way of the garden, the cross, and the grave. Nothing will dare to inflict so much pain—as the love which desires the richest and sweetest life of the object of its affection. "Whom the Lord loveth He chasteneth; and scourgeth every son whom He receiveth." Let us prepare then for coming hours of trial by doing as Abraham did.

(I) LET US LIVE BY THE WELL.—There is a great tendency among Christians to-day to magnify special places and scenes which have been associated with times of blessing; and to obtain from them a supply which they store up for their maintenance in after-days. But so many of these, and of others, are in danger of forgetting that instead of making an annual pilgrimage to the well, they might take up their abode beside it, and live there.

The water of that well speaks of the life of God, which is in Jesus Christ our Lord, and is stored up for us in the fathomless depths of the Word of God. The well is deep; yet can faith's bucket reach its precious contents, and bring them to thirsty lip and yearning heart.

One of the greatest blessings that can come to the soul is to acquire the habit of sinking wells into the depth that lieth under, and to draw water for itself. We are too much in the habit of drinking water which others have drawn; and too little initiated into the sacred science of drawing for ourselves.

It is my growing conviction that if Christians would not attempt to read so many chapters of the Bible daily, but would study what they do read more carefully, turning to the marginal references, reading the context, comparing Scripture with Scripture, endeavouring to get one or more complete thoughts of the mind of God, there would be a greater richness in their experience; more freshness in their interest in Scripture; more independence of men and means; and more real enjoyment of the Word of the living God. Oh for a practical realization of what Jesus meant when He said!—"The water that I shall give him shall be in him a well of water, springing up into everlasting life."

Oh, my readers, open your hearts to the teaching of the Holy Ghost. Rest content with nothing short of a deep and loving knowledge of the Bible. Ask that within you there may be a repetition of the old miracle, "when Israel sang this song: Spring up, O well; sing ye unto it" (Num. 21:17). Then "in the wilderness shall waters break out, and streams in the desert: and the parched ground shall become a pool, and the thirsty land springs of water" (Isa. 35:6, 7).

(2) LET US SHELTER BENEATH THE COVENANT.—Abraham was quiet from the fear of evil, because of Abimelech's oath. How much more sure and restful should be the believing soul, which shelters beneath that everlasting covenant which is "ordered in all things and sure." There are some Christians doubtful of their eternal salvation, and fearful lest they should ultimately fall away from grace and be lost, to whom this advice is peculiarly appropriate: "Live by the well of the oath."

In the eternity of the past, the Eternal Father entered into covenant with His Son, the terms of which covenant seem to have been on this wise. On the one hand our Lord pledged his complete obedience and His atoning death on behalf of all who should believe. And, on the other hand, the Father promised that all who should believe in Him should be delivered from the penalty of a broken law; should be forgiven; adopted into His family; and saved with an eternal salvation. This is but a crude and inadequate statement of mysteries so fathomless that the loftiest seraphs peer into them in vain. And yet it sets forth, in the babbling of human language, a truth of the utmost importance, behind which the weakest believer may securely shelter.

The one question is, Do you believe in Jesus Christ? Or, to put it still more simply, Are you willing that the Holy Ghost should create in you a living faith in the Saviour of men? *Would you believe if you could?* Is your will on God's side in this matter of faith? Are you prepared to surrender anything and everything that would hinder your simple-hearted faith in Jesus? If so, you may appropriate to yourself the blessings of the Covenant confirmed by the counsel and oath of God. Your faith may be weak; but it is faith in the embryo and germ. And as the Ark saved the squirrel as well as the elephant, so does the Covenant shelter the weakest and feeblest believer equally with the giant in faith.

This, then, becomes true of us, if we believe. We are forgiven; our name is inscribed on the roll of the saved; we are adopted into the family of God; we have within us the beginning of a life which is eternal as the life of God. "The mountains shall depart and the hills be removed; but My kindness shall not depart from thee, neither shall the covenant of My peace be removed, saith the Lord that hath mercy on thee" (Isa. 54:10). And shall not this comfort us amid many a heart-breaking sorrow? Nothing can break the bonds by which our souls are knit with the eternal God. "Although my house be not so with God; yet He hath made with me an everlasting covenant, ordered in all things and sure; for this is all my salvation, and all my desire, although He make it not to grow" (2 Sam. 23:5).

Rejoice in all the good things which the Lord thy God giveth thee. Plant thy trees; be comforted by their shade, and fed by their fruit. Listen to the ringing laughter of thine Isaac. Dread not the future; but trust the great love of God. Live by the well, and shelter beneath the covenant. So, if trial is approaching, thou shalt be the better able to meet it with a calm and strong heart.

we might well have exclaimed, "thou hast entered upon thy land of Beulah; thy sun shall no more go down, nor thy moon withdraw itself; before thee lie the sunlit years, in an unbroken chain of blessing." But this was not to be. And just at that moment, like a bolt out of a clear sky, there burst upon him the severest trial of his life. It is not often that the express trains of heaven are announced by warning bell, or falling signal; they dash suddenly into the station of the soul. It becomes us to be ever on the alert; for at such an hour and in such a guise as we think not, the Son of Man comes.

THE TRIAL TOUCHED ABRAHAM IN HIS TENDEREST POINT.—
It concerned his Isaac. Nothing else in the circumference of his life could have been such a test as anything connected with the heir of promise, the child of his old age, the laughter of his life. *His love was tested.* For love of God, he had done much. But at whatever cost, he had ever put God first, glad to sacrifice all, for very love of Him. For this he had torn himself from Charran. For this he had been willing to become a homeless wanderer; content if at the last he became an inmate of God's home. For this he had renounced the hopes he had built on Ishmael; driving him, as a scapegoat, into the wilderness to return no more. But, perhaps, if he had been asked if he felt that he loved God most of all, he would not have dared to say that he did. We can never gauge our love by feeling. The only true test of love is how much we are prepared to do for the one to whom we profess it. "He that hath My commandments, and keepeth them, he it is that loveth Me." But God knew how true and strong His child's love was, and that he loved Him best. So He put him to a supreme test, that all men might henceforth know that a mortal man could love God so much as to put Him first, though his dearest lay in the opposite scale of the balance of the heart. Would not you like to love God like this? Then tell Him you are willing to pay the cost, if only He will create that love within you. And, remember: though at first He may ask you to give up your Isaac to Him, it is only that you may take up your true position, and evince to the world your choice; for He will give your beloved back again from the altar on which you have laid him. "Take now thy son, thine only son Isaac, whom thou lovest, and offer him for a burnt-offering" (Gen. 22:2).

IT WAS ALSO A GREAT TEST OF HIS FAITH.—Isaac was the child of promise. "In Isaac shall thy seed be called." With

131

reiterated emphasis this lad had been indicated as the one essential link between the aged pair and the vast posterity which was promised them. And now the father was asked to sacrifice his life. It was a tremendous test to his faith. How could God keep His word, and let Isaac die? It was utterly inexplicable to human thought. If Isaac had been old enough to have a son who could perpetuate the seed to future generations, the difficulty would have been removed. But how could the childless Isaac die; and still the promise stand of a posterity through him, innumerable as stars and sand? One thought, however, as the Epistle to the Hebrews tells us, filled the old man's mind, "GOD IS ABLE." He "accounted that God was able to raise him up, even from the dead" (Heb. 11:19). He felt sure that somehow God would keep His word. It was not for him to reason how, but simply to obey. He had already seen Divine power giving life where all was as good as dead; why should it not do it again? In any case he must go straight on, doing as he was told, and calculating on the unexhausted stores in the secret hand of God. Oh for faith like this!—simply to believe what God says; assured that God will do just what He has promised; looking without alarm, from circumstances that threaten to make the fulfilment impossible, to the bare word of God's unswerving truthfulness. Surely this habit is not so impossible of attainment. Why then should we not begin to practise it, stepping from stone to stone, until we are far out from the shore of human expediency leaning on the unseen but felt arm of Omnipotence?

IT WAS A TEST OF ABRAHAM'S OBEDIENCE.—It was in the visions of the night that the word of the Lord must have come to him: and early the next morning the patriarch was on his way. The night before, as he lay down, he had not the least idea of the mission on which he would be started when the early beams of dawn had broken up the short Eastern night. But he acted immediately. We might have excused him if he had dallied with his duty; postponing it, procrastinating, lingering as long as possible. That, however, was not the habit of this heroic soul, which had well acquired the habit of instantaneity, one of the most priceless acquisitions for any soul ambitious of saintliness. "And Abraham rose up early in the morning" (*ver.* 3). No other hand was permitted to saddle the ass, or cleave the wood, or interfere with the promptness of his action. He "saddled his ass, and clave the wood for the burnt-offering, and rose up, and went unto the place of which

God had told him." This promptness was his safeguard. While the herdsman were beginning to stir, and the long lines of cattle were being driven forth to their several grazing grounds, the old man was on his way. I do not think he confided his secret to a single soul, not even to Sarah. Why should he? The lad and he would enter the camp again, when the short but awful journey was over. "I and the lad will go yonder and worship, and come again to you."

THIS TEST DID NOT OUTRAGE ANY OF THE NATURAL INSTINCTS OF HIS SOUL.—First of all, he was too familiar with God's voice to mistake it. Too often had he listened to it to make a mistake in this solemn crisis. And he was sure that God had some way of deliverance; which, though he might not be able to forecast it, would secure the sparing of Isaac's life. Besides, he lived at a time when such sacrifices as that to which he was called were very common; and he had never been taught decisively that they were abhorrent to the mind of his Almighty Friend. We must, in reading Scripture, remember that at first all God's servants were more or less affected by the religious notions that were current in their age; and we must not imagine that in all respects they were divested of the misconceptions that resulted from the twilight revelation in which they lived, but have since become dissipated before the meridian light of the Gospel. One of the first principles of that old Canaanitish religion demanded that men should give their first-born for their transgression, the fruit of their body for the sin of their soul. On the altars of Moab, and Phœnicia, and Carthage; nay, even in the history of Israel itself—this almost irrepressible expression of human horror at sin, and desire to propitiate God, found terrible expression. Not that fathers were less tender than now, but because they had a keener sense of the terror of unforgiven sin; they cowered before gods whom they knew not, and to whom they imputed a thirst for blood and suffering; they counted no cost too great to appease the awful demands which ignorance, and superstition, and a consciousness of sin, made upon them.

Perhaps Abraham had lately witnessed these rites; and as he did so, he had thought of Isaac, and wondered if he could do the same with him; and marvelled why such a sacrifice had never been demanded at his hands. And it did not, therefore, startle him when God said, "Take now thy son, and offer him up." He was to learn that whilst God demanded as much love as ever the heathen gave their cruel and imaginary deities, yet Heaven would not permit of human sacrifices or of offered sons. A Greater Sacrifice was to be made to put away sin. Abraham's obedience was, therefore, allowed to go up to a certain point, and then peremptorily stayed—that in all future time men might know that God would not demand, or permit, or accept human blood at their hands, much less the blood of a bright and noble lad; and that in such things He could have no delight.

Here let us ask ourselves whether we are of this same mind; holding our treasures with a loose hand; loving God most of all; prepared to obey Him at all costs; slaying our brightest hopes if God bid it—because so sure that He will not fail or deceive us. If so, may God give us this mind, and keep us in it, for His glory, and for the maturing of our own faith.

What those three days of quiet travelling must have been to Abraham, we can never know. It is always so much easier to act immediately and precipitately, than to wait through long days, and even years; but it is in this process of waiting upon God that souls are drawn out to a strength of purpose and nobility of daring, which become their sacred inheritance for all after-time. And yet, despite the patriarch's pre-occupation with his own special sorrow, the necessity was laid upon him to hide it under an appearance of resignation, and even gladsomeness; so that neither his son nor his servants might guess the agony which was gnawing at his heart.

At last, on the third day, he saw from afar the goal of his journey. God had informed him that He would tell him which of the mountains was the appointed spot of the sacrifice: and now probably some sudden conviction seized upon his soul, that an especial summit, which reared itself in the blue distance, was to be the scene of that supreme act in which he should prove that to his soul God was chiefest and best. Tradition, which seems well authenticated, has always associated that "mountain in the land of Moriah" with the place on which, in after days, stood the threshing floor of Araunah the Jebusite, and the site of Solomon's Temple; and there is a wonderful appropriateness in the fact that this great act of obedience took place on the very spot where hecatombs of victims and rivers of blood were to point to that supreme Sacrifice which this prefigured.

As soon as the mountain had loomed into view, Abraham said unto his young men: "Abide ye here with the ass; and I and the lad will go yonder and worship, and come again to you." What a significant expression, in this connection, is that word WORSHIP! It reflects the mood of the patriarch's mind. He was pre-occupied with that Being, at whose command he had gone forth on this sorrowful errand. He looked upon his God, at the moment when He was asking so great a gift, as only deserving adoration and worship. The loftiest sentiment that can fill the heart of man swayed his whole nature; and it seemed to him as if his costliest and dearest treasure was not too great to give to that great and glorious God who was the one object of his life.

It is of the utmost importance that we should emphasize the words of *assured confidence*, which Abraham addressed to his young men before he left them. "I and the lad will go yonder and worship, and come again to you." This was something more than unconscious prophecy: it was the assurance of an unwavering faith, that somehow or other God would interpose to spare his son; or at least, if necessary, to raise him from the dead. In any case Abraham was sure that Isaac and he would before long come again. It is this which so largely removes the difficulties that might otherwise obscure this act; and it remains to all time a most striking proof of the tenacity with which faith can cling to the promises of God. When once you have received a promise, cling to it as a sailor to a spar in the midst of the boiling waters. God is bound to be as good as His word. And even though He ask you to do the one thing that might seem to make deliverance impossible; yet if you dare to do it, you will find not only that you shall obtain the promise, but that you shall also receive some crowning and unexpected mark of His love.

THE INFLUENCE OF ABRAHAM'S BEHAVIOUR WAS FELT BY HIS SON.—He caught his father's spirit. We do not know how old he was; he was at least old enough to sustain the toil of a long march on foot, and strong enough to carry up hill the faggots, laid upon his shoulders by his father, But he gladly bent his youthful strength under the weight of the wood, just as through the *Via Dolorosa* a greater than he carried His cross. Probably this was not the first time that Abraham and Isaac had gone on such an errand; but it is beautiful to see the evident interest the lad took in the proceedings as they went, "both of them together."

At all previous sacrifices, Abraham had taken with him a lamb; but on this occasion Isaac's wondering attention was drawn to the omission of that constant appendage to their acts of sacrifice; and with a simplicity which must have touched Abraham to the quick, he said, "My father, behold the fire and the wood! but where is the lamb for a burnt-offering?" What a stab was this to that sorely-tried heart, which dared not even reveal the secret beneath which it bowed; and which eagerly caught at a subterfuge to enable it to postpone the answer. Thus with a gleam of prophetic insight, mingled with unwavering faith in Him for whose sake he was suffering, the father answered, "My son, God will Himself provide a lamb for a burnt-offering." So they went both of them together.

CAN WE WONDER THAT ABRAHAM SHRANK FROM DISCLOSING ALL THE FACTS?—We all have our treasures whom we fondly love. We shudder at the remotest thought of losing them. With breaking hearts we watch the colour fade from the cheek of a darling child, or mark the slow progress of disease in some twin soul; but Abraham must submit to a keener test than these. Our dear ones depart in spite of all we do to keep them; but in Abraham's case there was this added anguish, that he was to inflict the blow. The last thought that Isaac would have of him would be, holding the uplifted knife; and even though the lad might be restored to him—yet would it not be a revelation to the young heart to discover that it was possible for his father to do to him an act of violence like that?

BUT AT LAST THE DISCOVERY COULD NO LONGER BE WITHHELD.—"They came to the place which God had told him of, and Abraham built an altar there, and laid the wood in order." Can you not see the old man slowly gathering the stones; bringing them from the furthest distance possible; placing them with a reverent and judicious precision; and binding the wood with as much deliberation as possible? But at last everything is complete; and he turns to break the fatal secret to the young lad who had stood wonderingly by. Inspiration draws a veil over that last tender scene—the father's announcement of his mission; the broken sobs; the kisses, wet with tears; the instant submission of the son, who was old enough and strong enough to rebel if he had had the mind. Then the binding of that tender frame; which, indeed, needed no compulsion, because the young heart had learned the secret of obedience and resignation. Finally, the lifting him to lie upon the altar, on the wood. Here was a spectacle which must have arrested the attention of heaven. Here was a proof of how much mortal man will do for the love of God. Here was an evidence of child-like faith which must have thrilled the heart of the Eternal God, and moved Him in the very depths of His being. Do you and I love God like this? Is He more to us than our nearest and dearest? Suppose they stood on this side, and He on that side: would we go with Him, though it cost us the loss of all? You think you would. Aye, it is a great thing to say. The air upon this height is too rare to breathe with comfort. The one explanation of it is to be found in the words of our Lord: "He that loveth father or mother, son or daughter, more than Me is not worthy of Me" (Matt. 10:37).

The blade was raised high, flashing in the rays of the morning sun; but it was not permitted to fall. With the temptation God also made a way of escape. "And the angel of the Lord called unto him out of heaven, and said, 'Abraham!'" With what avidity would that much-tried soul seize at anything that offered the chance of respite or of pause! and he said, his uplifted hand returning gladly to his side, "Here am I!" Would that we could more constantly live in the spirit of that response, so that God might always know where to find us; and so that we might be always ready to fulfil His will. Then followed words that spoke release and deliverance: "Lay not thine hand upon the lad, neither do thou anything unto him: for now I know that thou fearest God, seeing thou hast not withheld thy son, thine only son, from Me" (ver. 12).

When we have given our best and costliest to God, passing our gifts through the fire surrendering them to His will, He will give them back to us as gold refined—multiplied, as Job's belongings were. But it is also quite likely that He will not do so until we have almost lost all heart and hope. "Abraham called the name of that place Jehovah-Jireh," "The Lord will provide." And so it passed into a proverb, and men said one to another, "In the mount of the Lord deliverance shall be seen." It is a true word. Deliverance is not seen till we come to the mount of sacrifice. God does not provide deliverance until we have reached the point of our extremest need. It is when our Isaac is on the altar, and the knife is about to descend upon him, that God's angel interposes to deliver.

Near by the altar there was a thicket; and, as Abraham lifted up his eyes and looked around, he beheld a ram caught there by its horns. Nothing could be more opportune. He had wanted to show his gratitude, and the fulness of his heart's devotion; and he gladly went and took the ram, and offered him up for a burnt-offering instead of his son. Here, surely, is the great doctrine of substitution; and we are taught how life can only be preserved at the cost of life given. According to one of the early Church writers, there is a yet deeper mystery latent here; viz., that whilst Isaac represents the Deity of Christ, the ram represents His human nature, which became a sacrifice for the sins of the world. I am not sure that I would altogether accept this interpretation; because it is the Deity of Christ working through His humanity which gives value to His sacrifice; but all through this marvellous story there is an evident setting forth of the mysteries of Calvary.

Abraham's act enables us better to understand the sacrifice which God made to save us. The gentle submission of Isaac, laid upon the altar with throat bare to the knife, gives us a better insight into Christ's obedience to death. Isaac's restoration to life, as from the dead, and after having been three days dead in his father's purpose, suggests the resurrection from Joseph's tomb. Yet the reality surpasses the shadow. Isaac suffers with a clear apprehension of his father's presence. Christ, bereft of the consciousness of His Father's love, complains of His forsakenness. All was done that love could do to alleviate Isaac's anguish; but Christ suffered the rudeness of coarse soldiery, and the upbraidings of Pharisee and Scribe. Isaac was spared death; but Christ drank the bitter cup to its dregs.

Before they left the mountain brow, the angel of Jehovah once more addressed the patriarch. God had often promised; now for the first time He sware; and since He could swear by no greater He sware by Himself, and said: "By Myself have I sworn, because thou hast done this thing, and hast not withheld thy son, thine only son; that in blessing I will bless thee; and in multiplying I will multiply thy seed as the stars of heaven, and as the sand which is upon the sea shore; and thy seed shall possess the gate of his enemies; and in thy seed shall all the nations of the earth be blessed; because thou hast obeyed My voice" (ver. 16, 17). Think not, O soul of man that this is a unique and solitary experience. It is simply a specimen and pattern of God's dealings with all souls who are prepared to obey Him at whatever cost. After thou hast patiently endured, thou shalt receive the promise. The moment of supreme sacrifice shall be the moment of supreme and rapturous blessing. God's river, which is full of water, shall burst its banks, and pour upon thee a tide of wealth and grace. There is nothing, indeed, which God will not do for a man who dares to step out upon what seems to be the mist; though as he puts down his foot he finds it rock beneath him.

ALL WHO BELIEVE ARE THE CHILDREN OF FAITHFUL ABRAHAM.—We then, Gentiles though we are, divided from him by the lapse of centuries, may inherit the blessing that he won; and the more so as we follow closely in his steps. That blessing is for us if we will claim it. That multiplication of seed may be realized in our fruitfulness of service. That victory over all enemies may give us victory in all time of our temptation, and that blessing for all the nations of the earth may be verified again as we go forth into all the world telling the story of a Saviour's death.

From that eminence Abraham looked across the vale of centuries, and saw the day of Christ. He "saw it, and was glad" (John 8:56). With a new light in his heart, with a new composure on his face, talking much with Isaac of the vision which had broken upon his noble soul, Abraham returned to his young men. "And they rose up and went together to Beersheba, and Abraham dwelt at Beersheba;" but the halo of the vision lit up the common places of his life, as it shall do for us, when from the mounts of sacrifice we turn back to the lowlands of daily duty.

Machpelah, and its First Tenant

> *Give me a possession of a burying-place with you; that I may bury my dead out of my sight.*—Genesis 23 : 4.
>
> *"And Abraham buried Sarah, his wife, in the cave of the field of Machpelah, before Mamre."*
> —Genesis 23 : 19.

When Abraham came down the slopes of Mount Moriah, hand in hand with Isaac, fifty years of his long life still lay before him. Of those fifty years, twenty-five passed away before the event recorded in this chapter. What happened in those serene and untroubled years which lie between these two chapters, as a valley between two ridges of hills, we do not know. In all likelihood one year was as much as possible like another. Few events broke their monotony. The river of Abraham's life had passed the rapids and narrows of its earlier course, and now broadened into reaches of still water, over which its current glided with an almost imperceptible movement.

The changes that mark the progress of our year are unknown beneath those glorious skies which rain perpetual summer on the earth; and the equableness of the climate is symbolical of the equableness of the simple patriarchal life. The tending of vast flocks and herds; the perpetual recurrence of birth, marriage, and death, among the vast household of slaves; the occasional interchange of hospitality with neighbouring clans; special days for sacrifice and worship;—these would be the most exciting episodes of that serene and calm existence, which is separated as far as possible from our feverish, broken lives. And yet, is there so very much that we can vaunt ourselves in, when we compare our days with those? True, there was not the railway; the telegraph wire; the journal; the constant interchange of news. But perhaps life may more fully attain its ideal, and fulfil its purpose, when its moments and hours are not dissipated by the constant intrusion of petty details, like those which for most of us make up the fabric of existence.

Perhaps we can never realize how much the members of such a household as Abraham's would be to one another. Through long, unbroken periods they lived together, finding all their society in one another. The course of pastoral life left ample leisure for close personal intercourse; and it was inevitable that human lives spent under such circumstances should grow together; even as trees in a dense wood, wherein they sometimes became so entangled and entwined that no human ingenuity can disentangle one from another. Thus it must have happened that the loss through death of one loved and familiar face would leave a blank never to be filled, and scarcely ever to be forgotten. We need not wonder, therefore, that so much stress is laid upon the death of Sarah, the chief event of those fifty years of Abraham's life; nor need we regret that such ample details are given of her death and burial; since they enable us to get a glimpse of the patriarch, and see if he has altered at all during the quarter of a century which has passed over him.

(1) WE ARE FIRST ARRESTED BY ABRAHAM'S TEARS.—"And Sarah died in Kirjath-Arba; the same is Hebron in the land of Canaan." Abraham seems to have been away from home, perhaps at Beersheba, when she breathed her last; but he came at once "to mourn for Sarah, and to weep for her." This is the first time we read of Abraham weeping. We do not read that he wept when he crossed the Euphrates, and left for ever home and kindred. There is no record of his tears when tidings came to him that his nephew Lot was carried into captivity. He does not seem to have bedewed his pathway to Mount Moriah with the tears of his heart. But now that Sarah is lying dead before him, the fountains of his grief are broken up.

What made the difference?—Ah! there is all the difference between *doing* God's will and *suffering* it. So long as we have something to do for God—whether it be a toilsome march; or a battle; or a sacrifice—we can keep back our tears, and bear up with fortitude. The multiplicity of our engagements turns away our attention from our griefs. But when all is over; when there is nothing more do do; when we are left with the silent dead, requiring nothing more at our hands; when the last office is performed, the last flower arranged, the last touch given—then the tears come.

It is not wonderful that Abraham wept.—Sarah had

been the partner of his life for seventy or eighty years. She was the only link to the home of his childhood. She alone could sympathize with him when he talked of Terah and Nahor, or of Haran and Ur of the Chaldees. She alone was left of all who thirty years before had shared the hardships of his pilgrimage. As he knelt by her side, what a tide of memories must have rushed over him of their common plans, and hopes, and fears, and joys! He remembered her as the bright young wife; as the fellow-pilgrim; as the childless persecutor of Hagar; as the prisoner of Pharaoh and Abimelech; as the loving mother of Isaac; and every memory would bring a fresh rush of tears.

There are some who chide tears as unmanly, unsubmissive, unchristian. They would comfort us with a chill and pious stoicism, bidding us meet the most agitating passages of our history with rigid and tearless countenance. With such the spirit of the Gospel, and of the Bible, has little sympathy. We have no sympathy with a morbid sentimentality; but we may well question whether the man who cannot weep can really love; for sorrow is love, widowed and bereaved—and where that is present, its most natural expression is in tears. Religion does not come to make us unnatural and inhuman; but to purify and ennoble all those natural emotions with which our manifold nature is endowed. Jesus wept. Peter wept. The Ephesian converts wept on the neck of the Apostle whose face they thought they were never to see again. Christ stands by each mourner, saying, "Weep, my child; weep, for I have wept."

Tears relieve the burning brain, as a shower the electric clouds. Tears discharge the insupportable agony of the heart, as an overflow lessens the pressure of the flood against the dam. Tears are the material out of which heaven weaves its brightest rainbows. Tears are transmuted into the jewels of better life, as the wounds in the oyster turn to pearls. Happy, however, is that man who, when he weeps for his departed, has not to reproach himself with unkindnesses and bitter words. We cannot always understand what makes people weep, when we stand with them on the loose earth beside the open grave. In many cases this sorrow is due to pure affection; in some cases, however, there is an additional saltness in their tears, because of unspoken regret. "I wish that I had not acted so: that I could recall those words: that I had had another opportunity of expressing the love I really felt, but hid: that I had taken more pains to curb myself; to be gentle, loving, endearing, and endeared. Oh for one hour of explanation and confession and forgiveness!" Let us see to it that we may never have to drink such bitter ingredients in the cup of our bereavement; and that we may not, let us not fail to give expression to those nobler feelings which often strive within our breasts, but which we too often repress.

And if some should read these words whose tears are the more bitter because they themselves are unsubmissive, let such remember that where they cannot feel resigned, they must will to be resigned, putting their will on God's side in this matter; asking Him to take it and fashion it according to His own; and remembering that our only province is with the will. This is all God asks; and if this is right with Him, He will subdue every other thought, and bring the whole being into a state of glad acquiescence. "I delight to do Thy will, O my God." "Though He slay me, yet will I trust Him!"

(2) NOTICE ABRAHAM'S CONFESSION.—"Abraham stood up from before his dead, and spake unto the sons of Heth, saying, I am a stranger and a sojourner with you; give me a possession of a burying-place with you" (Gen. 23 : 3, 4). See how sorrow reveals the heart. When all is going well, we wrap up our secrets; but when sorrow rends the vail, the *arcana* of the inner temple are laid bare! To look at Abraham as the great and wealthy patriarch, the emir, the chieftain of a mighty clan, we cannot guess his secret thoughts. He has been in the land for sixty-two years; and surely by this time he must have lost his first feelings of loneliness. He is probably as settled and naturalized as any of the princes round. So you might think, until he is widowed of his beloved Sarah! Then, amidst his grief, you hear the real man speaking his most secret thought: "I am a stranger and a sojourner with you."

These are very remarkable words; and they were never forgotten by his children. Speaking of the land of promise, God said, through Moses, to the people, "The land shall not be sold for ever; for ye are strangers and sojourners with Me." When David and his people made splendid preparations to build the Temple, as their spokesman he said, "Who am I, and what is my people, that we should be able to offer so willingly? for all things come of Thee; for we are strangers before Thee and sojourners, as were all our fathers. Our days on the earth are as a shadow, and there is none abiding." And, further, in one of his matchless Psalms, he pleads, "Hear my prayer, O Lord!

Hold not Thy peace at my tears; for I am a stranger with Thee, and a sojourner, as all my fathers were." So deeply had those words of Abraham sunk in the national mind, that the Apostle inscribes them over the cemetery where the great and the good of the Jewish nation lie entombed: "These all died in faith, not having received the promises, but having seen them afar off, and were persuaded of them, and embraced them, and confessed that they were strangers and pilgrims on the earth" (Heb. 11:13).

We may ask what it was that maintained this spirit in Abraham for so many years. There is but one answer: "They that say such things declare plainly that they seek a country" (Heb. 11:14). That country is never looked upon by the sun, or watered by the rivers of the earth, or refreshed by the generous dews. It is the better country, even the heavenly; the city which hath foundations, whose builder and maker is God; the land that needs neither sun nor moon, because the Lord God and the Lamb are the light thereof. Uprooted from the land of his birth, the patriarch could never take root again in any earthly country; and his spirit was always on the alert, eagerly reaching out towards the city of God, the home where only such royal souls as his can meet their peers, and find their rest. He refused to be contented with anything short of this; and, therefore, God was not ashamed to be called his God, because He had prepared for him a city. How this elevation of soul shames some of us! In our better moments we say that we are "the burgesses of the skies"; but our conversation is not in heaven, in our practical ordinary daily life. We profess to look for a city; but we take good care to make for ourselves an assured position among the citizens of this world. We affect to count all things dross; but the eagerness with which, muck-rake in hand, we strive to heap together the treasures of earth is a startling commentary upon our words.

(3) NOTICE ABRAHAM'S FAITH.—Men are wont to bury their dead besides their ancestors. The graves of past generations are the heritage of their posterity. By them rather than by the habitations of the living do tribes and races of men find their resting-place. The American loves to visit the quiet English churchyard where his fathers lie. The Jew elects in old age to journey to Palestine, that dying he may be buried in soil consecrated by the remains of his race. And it may be that Abraham first thought of that far distant grave in Charran, where Terah and Haran lay buried. Should he take Sarah thither? "No,"

thought he, "that country, has no claim upon me now. The only land, indeed, on which I have a claim is this wherein I have been a stranger. Here in after-days shall my children live. Here the generations that bear my name shall spread themselves out as the sands on the sea shore, and as the stars in the midnight sky. It is meet, therefore, that I should place our grave, in which Sarah their mother, and I their father, shall lie, in the heart of the land—to be a nucleus around which our descendants shall gather in all coming time. What though, as God has told me, four hundred years of suffering and furnace fire must pass, yet my children shall ultimately come hither again: and I will hold the land in pledge, against their coming, sure that it shall be as God has said!"

It is very beautiful to remark the action of Abraham's faith in this matter; and to see its outcome in his utter refusal to receive the land as a gift from any hand but that of God. When the chieftains to whom he made his appeal heard it, they instantly offered him the choice of their sepulchre affirming that none of them would withhold his sepulchre from so mighty a prince. And afterwards, when he sought their intercession with Ephron the son of Zohar, for the obtaining of the cave of Machpelah, which was at the end of his field, and Ephron proposed to give it him in the presence of the sons of his people, Abraham steadfastly refused. It was all his as the gift of God; it would be all his some day in fact; and in the meanwhile he would purchase the temporary use of that which he could never accept as a gift from any but his Almighty Friend.

And so after many courteous speeches, in the dignified manner which still prevails amongst Orientals, "the field and the cave, and all the trees, were made sure unto Abraham for a possession in the presence of the children of Heth, before all that went in at the gate of his city" (Gen. 23:17, 18). Their witness had the same binding effect in those rude days as legal documents have in our own.

There Abraham buried Sarah; there Isaac and Ishmael buried Abraham; there they buried Isaac, and Rebecca his wife; there Jacob buried Leah; and there Joseph buried Jacob his father; and there in all likelihood, guarded by the jealous Moslem, untouched by the changes and storms that have swept around their quiet resting-place, those remains are sleeping still, holding that land in fee, and anticipating the time when on a larger and more prominent scale the promise of God to Abraham shall be accomplished.

Not yet has the Divine promise been fully realized. The children of Abraham have possessed the Land of Promise for "but a little while" (Isa. 63:18). For long ages their adversaries have held sway there. But the days are hastening on when once more God will set His hand to gather His chosen people from all lands; and the infidel shall no longer desecrate those sacred spots; but once again shall the hills, and valleys, and pasture lands of Palestine come into the possession of the seed of Abraham, the friend of God.

23

The Soul's Answer to the Divine Summons

I will go!—Genesis 24:58.

Carry back your mind for thirty-seven centuries. The soft light of an Oriental sunset falls gently on the fertile grazing grounds watered by the broad Euphrates; and as its gloom lights up all the landscapes dotted by flocks, and huts, and villages, it irradiates with an especial wealth of colour the little town of Haran, founded one hundred years before by Terah, who, travelling northwards from Ur, resolved to go no further. The old man was smarting keenly at the recent loss of his youngest son, and after him the infant settlement was named. And so in time houses were built, and girdled by a wall in Oriental style. There Terah died, and thence the caravan had started at the command of God across the terrible desert, for the unknown Land of Promise. One branch of the family, however—that of Nahor —lived there still. His son, Bethuel, was the head; and in that family, at the time of which I speak, there was at least a mother; a brother named Laban; and a daughter in the first flush of girlish beauty, Rebecca.

It is Rebecca who occupies the central place in the pastoral scene before us. All her young life had been spent in that old town. Daughter of the Sheikh though she was, yet she was not kept in that listless indolence which dares not soil the fingers with honest work. She could make savoury meat, and tend the flocks, as her niece Rachel did in after-years on that same spot, and carry her pitcher gracefully poised upon her shoulder. She knew by name all the people who dwelt in that little town; and she had heard of those of her kindred who before her birth had gone beyond the great desert, and of whom hardly a word had travelled back for so many years. She little guessed the greatness of the world, and of her place in it; and in her wildest dreams she never thought of doing more than living and dying within the narrow limits of her native place. Elastic in step, modest in manner, pure in heart, amiable and generous, with a very fair face, as the sacred story tells us—how little did she imagine that the wheel of God's providence was soon to catch her out of her quiet home, and whirl her into the mighty outer world that lay beyond the horizon of desert sand.

On a special evening a stranger halted at the well, without the little town. He had with him a stately caravan of ten camels, each richly laden, and all bearing traces of long travel. There the little band waited, as if not knowing what next to do. Its leader was probably the good Eliezer, the steward of Abraham's house, who had come there on a solemn commission from his master. Abraham was now advanced in years. Isaac his son was forty years of age, and the old man longed to see him suitably married; and though his faith never doubted that God would fulfil His promise of the seed, yet he was desirous of clasping in his aged arms the second link between him and his posterity. He had therefore bound his trusty servant by a double oath: first, that he would not take a wife for Isaac from the daughters of the Canaanites around them, but from his own kith and kin at Haran; and secondly, that he would never be an accomplice to Isaac's return to the land which he had left. This solemn oath was lit up by the assurance of the old man, that the Lord God of heaven, who took him from his father's house and the land of his kindred, would send His angel before him, and would crown his mission with success.

Having arrived at the city-well towards nightfall,—"even, the time that women go out to draw water"—the devout leader asked that God would send him "good speed," addressing the Almighty as the Lord God of his master Abraham, and pleading that in prospering his way He would show kindness to his master. The simplicity and trustfulness of his prayer are very beautiful; and are surely the reflection of the piety which reigned in that vast encampment gathered around the wells of Beersheba, and which was the result of Abraham's own close walk with God. There would be less fault to find with servants in the present day, if they were treated as servants were once treated—as souls rather than hands; and if they were encouraged to imitate, because they had learned to admire, the character of those with whom they live in such close contact. Alas that servants in Christian homes often find so little to attract them to the godliness which is professed, but scantily practised!

It is our privilege to talk with God about everything in life. The minutest things are not too small for Him who numbers the hairs of our heads. No day can we afford to spend, without asking that He should send us good speed. Well would it be for us, as we stand by the well at morning, or at eventide, to commit our way unto the Lord, trusting that He should bring it to pass. And if this be true of ordinary days, how much more of those days which decide destiny, which are the watershed of life, and in which plans are concluded which may affect all after-years! Nor is it wrong for us to ask a sign from God, if by this we mean that He would permit the circumstances of our daily lot to indicate His will: to confirm by inner inspiration from Himself, and to embody, in fact, that which has already been impressed upon our own conscience. We have no right to ask for signs for the gratification of a morbid curiosity; but we are justified in asking for the concurrence of outward providence indicating the will of God. It was a holy and a happy inspiration that led the godly servant to ask that the damsel, who responded with courteous alacrity to his request for water, should be she whom God had appointed as a bride for his master's son; and it happened to him as it will always happen to those who have learned to trust like little children, that "before he had done speaking," his answer was waiting by his side.

We need not tell in detail all that followed: the gifts of heavy jewellery; the reverent recognition of God's goodness in answering prayer, as the man bowed down his head and worshipped the Lord; the swift run home; the admiration of mother and brother at the splendid gifts; the breathless telling of the unexpected meeting; the proffered hospitality of Laban, whose notions of hospitality were quickened by his keen eye for gain, and who spoke the words of welcome with extra heat because he saw the rich lading of the camels; the provision of straw and provender for the camels, of water for the feet of the weary drivers, and of food for their leader, and the refusal to eat until his errand was unravelled and its purpose accomplished; the story, told in glowing words, of Abraham's greatness; the narrative of the wonderful way in which the speaker had been led, and Rebecca indicated; the final request that her relatives would deal kindly and truly in the matter; and their unhesitating and swift consent in words that drew the old servant prostrate to the ground in holy ecstasy as he worshipped the Lord. "Behold," they said, "Rebecca is before thee; take her and go: and let her be thy master's wife, as the Lord hath spoken."

Then from his treasures he brought forth jewels of silver and jewels of gold, and raiment with which to deck

Rebecca's fair form; her mother and Laban also received precious things to their hearts' desire. "Then they did eat and drink, he and the men that were with him, and tarried all night." In the early dawn, refusing all invitation to further waiting, Abraham's steward started back again, carrying with him Rebecca and her nurse; and through the fragrant morning air the blessings of that little cluster of friendly hearts were wafted to her ear, as seated on her camel, and wrapped in a dream of girlish hope and wonder, she caught the last voice from her home. "They addressed Rebecca and said unto her, Thou art our sister: be thou the mother of thousands of millions; and let thy seed possess the gate of those which hate them."

We must thus pass over the details of this story, which carries on its forefront the stamp of inspiration and of truth; suffice it to say that it has no superior in this book for its rich, soft, placid style. It is full of those touches of nature which make all men kin, and which move them everywhere alike. Let us now elict two or three further lessons to illustrate by it the Divine summons, and the answer of the soul.

(1) A LESSON TO THOSE WHO CARRY THE SUMMONS OF GOD.—*Let us saturate our work with prayer.*—Like his master, the servant would not take a single step without prayer. Not that he always spoke aloud. No one would have known that the old man prayed as he stood there by the well. Nor did he arbitrarily dictate to God; but he threw the whole responsibility of the matter upon Him who had ever shown Himself so true a Friend to his beloved master. He had a most difficult thing to do, in which strong chances were running against him. Was it likely that a young girl would care to leave her home to cross the vast expanse of sand in company with himself, a complete stranger, and to become the wife of one whom she had never seen? "Peradventure the woman will not follow me!" and if she were willing, her relatives might not be; but he prayed, and prayed again, and God's good speed crowned his errand with complete success.

We too are sometimes sent on very unlikely errands, Humanly speaking, our mission seems likely to prove a failure: but those who trust in God have not the word "failure" in their vocabulary. Their hearts are centres from which the fragrance of silent prayer is ever exhaling into the presence of God. They succeed where they seem menaced with certain disappointment. Christian worker! never start on any mission for God, whether to an individual soul or to a congregation, without the prayer, "Send me good speed this day."

We must also wait upon God for direction.—Abraham's steward asked that the chosen bride should be willing to draw water for his camels. A trifle this must seem to some; and yet it was a true test for a girl's nature. It showed a ready kindness of heart, which was prepared to outrun the requirements of conventional politeness. It indicated a nature in which haughty pride had no place. Is it not a fact that in such trivial, unstudied acts there is a sure index of character? Very often God's servants make great mistakes; because they force themselves on souls, not living in the will of God, not seeking the indication of His bidding, not waiting until He should open the door of circumstance into some new life. We do not always realize the solemn mystery that surrounds each human soul; or the depths into which all spiritual consciousness may have receded; or the thick cake of worldliness and carelessness which may have crusted over the sensibilities of the being. God only understands all this; and we should do very wisely to wait expectantly and trustfully for Him to open up the way of access into the citadel of the heart. We may be sure that in this God will not fail us, but that whilst we are speaking He will hear and answer.

Let us say much in praise of our Master.—It is beautiful to notice how eloquent the old man is about his master. He does not say one word about himself, or extol himself in any way, so absorbed was he in the story of his absent, distant lord. Was not this also characteristic of the Apostles, who preached not themselves, but Christ Jesus the Lord; and whose narratives are like colourless glass, only letting His glory through? Alas! that we so obtrude ourselves, that men go away talking of us. Let us lose ourselves, in our theme. And whilst we show the jewels of Christian character in our own deportment, let the theme of our message be: "The Lord Jehovah hath greatly blessed our Master, Christ, and has given Him a name which is above every name; and has raised Him to His own right hand in the heavenly places, far above all principality and power, and every name that is named: and He is worthy to receive power, and riches, and strength, and honour, and glory, and blessing." And when success attends your words, be sure to give all the glory to Him from whom it has come.

(2) THE SUMMONS ITSELF was a call to a simple, penniless girl to ally herself in marriage to one of the wealthiest and noblest of earth's aristocracy. It was not sent because of

her worth, or wealth, or beauty; but because it was so willed in the heart and counsel of Abraham. Such a call is sent to every soul that hears the Gospel. In yonder azure depths lives the great Father God. He has one Son, His only-begotten and well-beloved. He has resolved to choose from amongst men those who as one Church shall constitute His bride for ever. He sends this call to you, not because you are worthy, or wealthy, or beautiful; but because He has so willed it in the counsel of His own heart: and He longs that you shall be willing to detach yourself from all that you hold dear. This is His message: "Hearken, O daughter, and consider, and incline thine ear! forget also thine own people and thy father's house: so shall the King greatly desire thy beauty: for He is thy Lord; and worship thou Him" (Ps. 45:10, 11).

And if that call is obeyed, thou shalt lose thine own name, sinner, in His name; thou shalt be arrayed in His fair jewels; thou shalt share His wealth; thou shalt sit down with Him on His throne; all things shall be thine. Wilt thou go with this Man? Wilt thou leave all to be Christ's? Wilt thou give thine unseen Lover thine heart, to be His for ever? Come and put yourself under the convoy of the blessed Holy Spirit, who pleads the cause of Jesus, as did Abraham's servant that Isaac; and let Him conduct you where Jesus is.

(3) HOW TO DEAL WITH THIS SUMMONS.—*We must find room for it.*—"Come in, thou blessed of the Lord; wherefor standest thou without? for I have prepared a house and room." The Master saith, "Where is the guest-chamber?" There was no room for Christ in the inn: but we must make room for Him in the heart; or, at least, we must be willing that He should make room for Himself.

We must bear witness.—"The damsel ran, and told them of her mother's house." As soon as you have heard the call, and received the jewels of promise, which are the earnest of your inheritance, you must go home to your friends and tell them what great things the Lord hath done for you.

We must not procrastinate, or confer with flesh and blood.—Men, and circumstances, would fain defer our starting on pilgrimage. This is Satan's method of breaking off the union for ever. There must be no dallying or delay: but when the enquiry is put to us, "Wilt thou go with this man?" we must promptly and swiftly answer, "I will go."

The journey was long and toilsome; but all the way the heart of the young girl was sustained by the tidings told her by the faithful servant, who beguiled the weary miles with stories of the home to which she was journeying, and the man with whom her life was to be united—"Whom having not seen, she loved; and in whom, though she saw him not, she rejoiced." She already loved him, and ardently longed to see him.

One evening the meeting came. Isaac had gone forth to meditate at eventide, sadly lamenting the loss of his mother, eagerly anticipating the coming of his bride, and interweaving all with holy thought. And when he lifted up his eyes across the pastures, lo, the camels were coming, and the two young souls leapt to each other. Happy meeting! which made Rebecca oblivious to all the trials and hardships of her journey, and the loss of her friends. Was it not also an emblem of the moment when the work of the Holy Spirit, our gracious Conductor, will conclude in the presence of our Lord, the true Bridegroom of saintly hearts, and we shall see his face, to be for ever with Him, going no more out for ever?

And after a while in that silent home, there was again the prattle of childish voices; and for several years the patriarch rejoiced in the presence of his grandchildren, to whom he would tell the history of the past, on which his aged soul loved to dwell. And of one narrative those lads would never tire; that which told how their father had once climbed the summit of Moriah, to be, as it were, raised from the dead.

24

Gathered to his People

These are the days of the years of Abraham's life which he lived; an hundred, threescore, and fifteen years. Then Abraham gave up the ghost, and died in a good old age, an old man, and full of years; and was gathered to his people.—Genesis 25:8.

No human name can vie with Abraham's for the widespread reverence which it has evoked amongst all races throughout all time. The pious Jew looked forward to reposing, after death, in the bosom of Father Abraham. The fact of descent from him was counted by thousands sufficient to secure them a passport into heaven. Apostles so opposite as Paul and James united in commending his example to the imitation of primitive Christians, in an age which had seen the Lord Jesus Himself. The mediaeval Church canonized Abraham alone among Old Testament worthies, by no decree, but by popular consent. Devout Mohammedans reverence his name as second only to that of their prophet. What was the secret of this widespread renown? It is not because he headed one of the greatest movements of the human family; nor yet because he evinced manly and intellectual vigour; nor because he possessed vast wealth. It was rather the remarkable nobility and grandeur of his religious life that has made him the object of veneration to all generations of mankind.

At the basis of his character was a mighty Faith.— "Abraham believed God." In that faith he left his native land, and travelled to one which was promised, but not clearly indicated. In that faith he felt able to let Lot choose the best he could for himself; because he was sure that none could do better for himself than God was prepared to do for the one who trusted Him. In that faith he waited through long years, sure that God would give him the promised child. In that faith he lived a nomad life, dwelling in tents, and making no attempt to return to the settled country from which he had come out. Indeed, his soul was consumed with the passionate expectancy of the city of God. In that faith he was prepared to offer Isaac, and buried Sarah.

Do not suppose that his faith dwelt alone. On the contrary, it bore much fruit; for if we test him by those catalogues of the fruits of faith which are provided in the New Testament, we shall find that he manifested them each and all. Take, for instance, the chain of linked graces enumerated in the Second Epistle by the Apostle Peter; a kind of golden ladder, stretched across the chasm between heaven and earth, and uniting them.

To Faith he added Virtue, or Manly Courage.—What could have been more manly than the speed with which he armed his trained servants; or than the heroism with which he, with a train of undisciplined shepherds, broke on the disciplined bands of Assyria, driving them before him as the chaff before the whirlwind, and returning victorious down the long valley of the Jordan?

And to Manly Courage he added Knowledge.—All his life he was a student in God's college of divinity. Year by year fresh revelations of the character and attributes of God broke upon his soul. He grew in the knowledge of God and the Divine nature, which at the first had been to him a *terra incognita*. An unknown country grew beneath his gaze; as he climbed through the years into closer fellowship with God, and from the summit looked down upon its lengths and breadths, its depths and heights, its oceans, mountain-ranges, and plains.

And to Knowledge he added Temperance, or Self-Control. —That he was master of himself is evident from the way in which he repelled the offer of the King of Sodom; and curbed his spirit amid the irritations caused by Lot's herdsmen. The strongest spirits are those which have the strongest hand upon themselves, and are able therefore, to do things which weaker men would fail in. There is no type of character more splendid than that of the man who is master of himself, because he is the servant of God; and who can rule others rightly because he can rule himself well.

And to Temperance, Patience.—Speaking of him, the voice of New Testament inspiration affirms that he "patiently endured" (Heb. 6:15). No ordinary patience was that which waited through the long years, not murmuring or complaining, but prepared to abide God's time; weaned from the breasts of earthly consolation and help, and quieted after the manner of the Psalmist, who said, "I have quieted myself as a child that is weaned of his mother:

155

my soul is even as a weaned child. Let Israel hope in the Lord from henceforth and for ever" (Ps. 131:2, 3).

And to his Patience he added Godliness.—One of his chief characteristics was his piety—a constant sense of the presence of God in his life, and a love and devotion to Him. Wherever he pitched his tent, there his first care was to rear an altar. Shechem, Hebron, Beersheba—alike saw these tokens of his reverence and love. In every time of trouble he turned as naturally to God as a child to its father; and there was such holy intercourse between his spirit and that of God, that the name by which he is now best known throughout the East is "THE FRIEND"— a name which he holds *par excellence,* and which has almost overshadowed the use of that name by which we know him best.

And to Godliness he added Brotherly Kindness.—Some men who are devoted towards God are lacking in the tenderer qualities towards those most closely knit with them in family bonds. Not so was it with Abraham. He was full of affection. Beneath the calm exterior and the erect bearing of the mighty chieftain there beat a warm and affectionate heart. Listen to that passionate cry, "Oh that Ishmael might live before Thee!" Remember God's own testimony to the affection he bore towards Isaac— "Thy son, thine only son, whom thou lovest." Abraham's nature therefore may be compared to those ranges of mighty hills, whose summits rear themselves above the region of storms, and hold converse with the skies; whilst their lower slopes are clothed with woods and meadows, where homesteads nestle and bright children string their necklaces of flowers with merry laughter.

And to Brotherly Kindness he added Charity, or Love.— In his dealings with men he could afford to be generous, open-hearted, open-handed; willing to pay down the large price demanded for Machpelah's cave without haggling or complaint; destitute of petty pride; affable, courteous, able to break out into sunny laughter; right with God, and therefore able to shed upon men the rays of a genial, restful noble heart.

All these things were in him and abounded, and they made him neither barren nor unfruitful; they made his calling and election sure; they prepared for him an abundant entrance into the everlasting kingdom of God our Saviour. The thought that underlies the expression in the Greek ($\pi\lambda o\upsilon\sigma\acute{\iota}\omega\varsigma$ $\dot{\eta}$ $\epsilon\ddot{\iota}\sigma o\delta o\varsigma$) is richly significant. The words denote the welcome given by choral songs and joyous greetings to the conqueror who, laden with spoils, returned to his native city; and they indicate that for some favoured souls, at least, there is waiting on the threshold of the other world a welcome so exuberant, so boisterous in its unutterable joy, so royally demonstrative, as to resemble that given in all times to those who have conferred great benefits, or who have learnt the art of stirring the loyal devotion of their fellows. If such an entrance could be accorded to any one, certainly it would be to Abraham, when stooping beneath the weight of one hundred threescore and fifteen years, "he gave up the ghost, and died at a good old age. an old man, full of years, and was gathered to his people."

"Abraham gave up the ghost."—There was no reluctance in his death; he did not cling to life—he was glad to be gone; and when the angel-messenger summoned him, without a struggle, nay, with the readiness of glad consent, his spirit returned to God who gave it.

He was gathered to his people.—This cannot refer to his body; for that did not sleep beside his ancestors, but side by side with Sarah's. Surely then it must refer to his spirit. The world's grey fathers knew little of the future; but they felt that there was somewhere a mustering place of their clan, whither devout and holy souls were being gathered, one by one, so that each spirit, as it passed from this world, went to rejoin its people; the people from which it had sprung; the people whose name it bore; the people to which by its tastes and sympathies it was akin.

What a lovely synonym for death! To DIE is to rejoin our people; to pass into a world where the great clan is gathering, welcoming with shouts each new-comer through the shadows. Where are your people? I trust they are God's people; and if so, those that bear your name, standing on the other shore, are more numerous than the handful gathered around you here; many whom you have never known, but who know you; many whom you have loved and lost awhile; many who without you cannot be made perfect in their happiness. There they are, rank on rank, company on company, regiment on regiment, watching for your coming. Be sure you do not disappoint them! But remember, if your people are God's people, you cannot be gathered to them unless first in faith and love you are gathered to Him.

Little doubt had this noble man of the recognition of saintly spirits in the other world; and indeed, it is an untrue conception which has filled the future with strange spirits, unknowing and unknown. Heaven is not a prison with tier on tier of cells; but a HOME. And what is home without the recognition of love of fond hearts? So long as we read of David going to his child; of Paul anticipating the pleasure of meeting again his converts; of the women and disciples being able to recognize the appearance and the love of the Saviour amid the glory of the resurrection body—we may be prepared to believe, with the patriarch, that dying is re-union with those to whom in the deepest sense we are related. Spiritual affinities are for all time and for eternity, and will discover themselves through all worlds.

"And his sons, Isaac and Ishmael, buried him in the cave of Machpelah."—There were great differences between these two. Ishmael, the child of his slave: Isaac, of the wedded wife. Ishmael, the offspring of expediency: Isaac, of promise. Ishmael, wild and masterful, "the wild ass"; strongly marked in his individuality; proud, independent, swift to take an insult, swift to avenge it: Isaac, quiet and retiring, submissive and meek, willing to carry wood, to be kept in the dark, to be bound, to yield up his wells, and to let his wife govern his house. And yet all differences were wiped out in that moment of supreme sorrow; and coming from his desert fastnesses, surrounded by his wild and ruffian freebooters, Ishmael united with the other son of their common father, who had displaced him in his inheritance, and who was so great a contrast to himself; but all differences were smoothed out in that hour.

Many ancient chieftains may have been gathered by that ancient cave, to join in one last act of respect to the mighty prince who had dwelt amongst them for so long. Amid the wail of the women, and the dirge which even to this day tells of sorrow for departed worth in Eastern lands—borne by a band of his trusted retainers, whilst a vast concourse of the camp stood wrapped in reverent silence around—the remains of the man who had dared to trust God at all costs, and who with pilgrim steps had traversed so many weary miles, were solemnly laid beside the dust of Sarah, his faithful wife. There, in all probability, they rest even to this day, and thence they will be raised at the coming of the King.

Out of materials which were by no means extraordinary, God built up a character with which He could hold fellowship as friend with friend; and a life which has exerted a profound influence on all after-time. It would seem as if He can raise any crop He chooses, when the soil of the heart and life are entirely surrendered to Him. Why should not we henceforth yield ourselves utterly to His divine husbandry, asking Him to fulfil in us the good pleasure of His goodness, and the work of faith with power? Only let us trust Him fully, and obey Him instantly and utterly; and as the years pass by, they shall witness results which shall bring glory to God in the highest, whilst they fill us with ceaseless praise.